"This is the book I have been waiting for to best introduce individuals and groups to mindfulness-based ways of navigating the fullness of life. Thomas Roberts is a masterful guide who weaves together decades of experience personally practicing mindfulness and therapeutically being with others through the agony, ecstasy, and boredom of everyday life. Roberts' guide to being present to mind and body within the flow of our lives should be become a model and a standard in the quickly expanding world of mindfulness research and applications."

—Greg Johanson, Ph.D., coauthor of *Grace Unfolding* and founding trainer of The Hakomi Institute

"Finally, a book that breaks down complex mindfulness concepts into easy to understand modules! Roberts masterfully guides you through many user-friendly techniques, making them much simpler to incorporate into everyday life. An excellent resource for beginners as well as seasoned practitioners."

—Niloufer Merchant, Ed.D., licensed psychologist and professor at St. Cloud State University in St. Cloud, MN

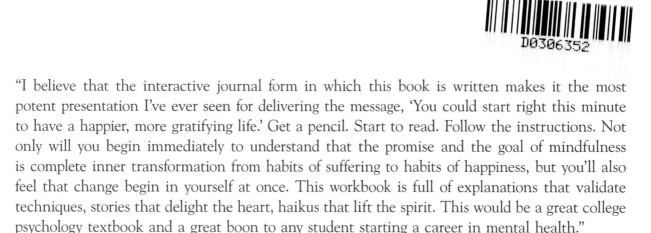

D0306352

"I believe that the interactive journal form in which this book is written makes it the most potent presentation I've ever seen for delivering the message, 'You could start right this minute to have a happier, more gratifying life.' Get a pencil. Start to read. Follow the instructions. Not only will you begin immediately to understand that the promise and the goal of mindfulness is complete inner transformation from habits of suffering to habits of happiness, but you'll also feel that change begin in yourself at once. This workbook is full of explanations that validate techniques, stories that delight the heart, haikus that lift the spirit. This would be a great college psychology textbook and a great boon to any student starting a career in mental health."

—Sylvia Boorstein, Ph.D., cofounder of Spirit Rock Meditation Center and author of *Happiness Is an Inside Job*

"*The Mindfulness Workbook* is filled with deep wisdom and many useful practices for living a mindful life. Read it, practice it, live it!"

> —Bob Salt, Ph.D., chair of the Human Development and Family Studies
> department at the University of Wisconsin-Stout

"*The Mindfulness Workbook* is a gem. I appreciate the reader-friendly format in which the thoughtful and valuable information is presented and am looking forward to the journey I am about to embark on by using this workbook!"

> —Sue Patton Thoele, author of *The Mindful Woman, The Courage To Be Yourself,*
> and *The Woman's Book of Soul*

THE MINDFULNESS WORKBOOK

a beginner's guide to overcoming fear & embracing compassion

THOMAS ROBERTS, LCSW, LMFT

New Harbinger Publications, Inc.

Publisher's Note

Distributed in Canada by Raincoast Books

Copyright © 2009 by Thomas Roberts
New Harbinger Publications, Inc.
5674 Shattuck Avenue
Oakland, CA 94609
www.newharbinger.com

FSC
Mixed Sources
Product group from well-managed
forests and other controlled sources
Cert no. SW-COC-002283
www.fsc.org
© 1996 Forest Stewardship Council

Acquired by Jess O'Brien; Cover design by Amy Shoup;
Edited by Jasmine Star; Text design by Tracy Carlson

Library of Congress Cataloging-in-Publication Data

Roberts, Thomas B.
  The mindfulness workbook : a beginner's guide to overcoming fear and embracing compassion / Thomas Roberts.
     p. cm.
  Includes bibliographical references.
  ISBN-13: 978-1-57224-675-1 (pbk. : alk. paper)
  ISBN-10: 1-57224-675-8 (pbk. : alk. paper) 1. Mind and body. 2. Fear. 3. Compassion. I. Title.
  BF161.R658 2009
  158.1--dc22

                                    2009038436

11 10 09

10 9 8 7 6 5 4 3 2 1   First printing

Contents

PART 3
Cultivating Mindfulness in All Aspects of Life

Acknowledgments

So many people's lives have crossed my path. Some have joined me, some have declined, some stayed a while and left, and all have made a profound impact on my life and soul. Many teachers have brought me to this point in my life. Some of them are formal teachers, like Dr. William Easson, who captivated my interested in the workings of the human mind. Others taught in different ways, like my brother Bob, who taught me that there was meaning beyond the sounds of silence; my sister Pam, who responded so selflessly; my sister Pat, whose death when I was a young boy awakened my journey; and Steve, a young client I encountered early in my career, who taught me to be comfortable with the strange and unpredictable.

My children, too, have been teachers, sent to me from beyond: Laura Shawn, whose insistence on the musical and wondrous is an inspiration; and Karl, who taught me that nothing this life dishes out is any reason to quit or give up. Some of my children arrived in my life at a later point and already on their journey: Laura K., who taught me that the size of a person resides in their heart and enthusiasm; and Stephanie, who taught me that gentle and quiet are deep and strong places.

For unwavering loyalty and support, I thank my office manager, Kathy R., whose steady patience reminds me to keep from complicating things, and that simple is good, and I also thank

Simon. Teachers also appeared in the form of my mistakes, which were life's corrective messages. I think I listened to most of them, and when I didn't, they kept coming back until I did.

Thank you to Jess O'Brien and Jess Beebe at New Harbinger Publications for your patience, suggestions, and encouragement throughout this most challenging journey. Your ideas have made their mark on this book. A special thank you to Jasmine Star, copy editor extraordinaire. From beginning to end, your skill and grace are infused throughout this book. You helped me create a book that is both readable and useful.

Then there is Kathy, my love, my strength, my friend, my inspiration. Your patience, love, and acceptance of me have touched me deeply. Without you standing by and paying attention to everything, including all of the details of daily life, I could not have written this book. Your honesty about which parts of my manuscript had more or less merit allowed me the freedom and creativity to explore during the writing process without having to worry if I made sense. Now that I think about it, I guess this also applies to how you have handled me in general. We are truly on a journey together, and I can't wait for the next episode. With spacious love and gratitude, I hold you in my heart always.

Introduction

Mindfulness is a way of *being* in the world. Being mindful means responding, not reacting, to the ever-present flow of events and experiences in your life with patience, openness, and compassion. Unfortunately, many of us have been conditioned to believe that we must protect ourselves from life and its experiences from a place of fear. This fear can harden you and influence the way you relate to yourself and your world, and ultimately create a great deal of suffering. Suffering doesn't lie in what occurs, it lies in resisting or fighting what occurs. But what if the true nature of the flow of your experiences is actually quite different from what you perceive and are reacting to? What if you could learn to observe the flow of your experiences without judgment, preconception, or distraction?

HOW THIS BOOK WILL HELP YOU

Your journey through this book will help you explore many aspects of your experience, including how you may be creating your own suffering. *The Mindfulness Workbook* will take you on a two-part journey. The first step (and you can't skip this step!) in cultivating mindfulness in your life is to become familiar with the ways you've created and maintained *mindless* living, and how fear and the strategies you've used to deal with fear are the foundation of your suffering. Know that you aren't alone in this; it's human nature to fall back on self-preserving, reactive emotional and behavioral strategies. For millennia these reactions were highly adaptive. But we live in a different world than our ancient forebears did, and we can all benefit from addressing the ways our mindless living strategies trip us up. For this reason, chapter 1 will get right to the heart of the matter and examine mindless living strategies. Once you learn to recognize these strategies, which I often refer to as *big deal mind*, you'll be able to catch yourself as you fall into them.

The second step, and the subject of the rest of the book, is learning ways to be in the presence of big deal mind without being drawn into its well-practiced repertoire of reactive thoughts and feelings. This opens the door to choosing a different response. Taking a step back from big deal mind will create the space needed for mindful responses, allowing you to develop and maintain mindful presence. The practices throughout the book will help you develop the mindful qualities of patience, openness, and compassion—qualities that will deepen your ability to choose mindful, meaningful responses rather than mindless reactions.

Throughout *The Mindfulness Workbook*, you'll work with these two pillars—understanding mindlessness and creating spaciousness—using them to deeply explore and address the core issues of your daily experiences. You'll examine many facets of your life and the world around you in order to awaken to the richness that exists amidst the everyday circumstances of your life. As you come to understand the sources of your suffering, you'll find the freedom to create and embrace the inherent joy of spacious awareness and the opening of your heart.

Creating spacious presence invites you to use what your life offers you—to view your experiences as your teacher, your scripture, your guru—laying the foundation for a greater sense of depth, meaning, and connection throughout all aspects of your life. Once you begin to soften to the flow of your experiences, your quality of life will greatly improve on its own accord. You'll experience greater emotional health, and it's likely your physical health will also improve. Your relationships will possess greater meaning and depth, and you may find that you grow spiritually, as well. As you clear away the mental and physical clutter that can consume your attention and energy, you'll open to the beauty, truth, and compassion that always surround us and that can suffuse our lives if we're open to that possibility.

Learning how to live mindfully isn't about getting some technique right, achieving a blissful state, or knowing the ultimate answers; it's about learning to let go of your fear and other patterns of habitual thought so you can stay present amidst your life as it unfolds. The mindful state isn't something you look for; it's already there and just needs space and a bit of attention to emerge.

A WAY OF RESPONDING

Mindfulness has become something of a buzzword, and as it's popularized, there's a risk of coming to see it as a commodity—something you can learn or get and be guaranteed wonderful outcomes. Be aware that mindfulness isn't an end state. First and foremost, it's a way of being with all of life's experiences, not just bliss, freedom, or abundance. It's an opening to the flow of your life. As you become aware of this flow, your mindful responses will be deeply connected to whatever is required in each given moment. Your responses will be fluid and dynamic, inviting you to relate to yourself, others, and the world around you with patience, openness, and compassion. Every time you're confronted with the unexpected, you have the opportunity to embrace the constant flow of your actual experiences, as opposed to thoughts, feelings, or judgments about those experiences, or attachment or aversion in regard to those experiences.

I emphasize the flow of your life rather than the here and now because every "now" is just a fleeting glimpse of the convergence of the immediate past and the immediate future. To discuss a "now" would imply that there's a moment frozen in space and time that you can call "now."

By applying mindfulness to this flow of your experiences, you'll build your own practice, and the benefits will manifest in ways that no one else can possibly define for you. When you allow mindful responses the space to emerge amidst this flow, you'll find you are *being* in ways that you may not have otherwise permitted.

For this reason, living mindfully can be rather unsettling, especially at first. Trappist monk Thomas Merton, who was deeply interested in interreligious understanding, developed a concept of contemplation that aligns with this view of mindfulness. In *New Seeds of Contemplation* (1972), he wrote that we must be careful not to look at contemplation as an escape from conflict or other difficulties in life. Contemplative practices often awaken unsettling feelings and deep, startling questions that can provoke doubt and uncertainty. Merton maintained that contemplation isn't a painkiller—that any difficulty you encounter is in and of itself your path and presents an opportunity to awaken to a more genuine self, and more genuine life experiences, as a result. The work lies in how you use your struggles to deepen your connection to your true self and your true experience. Be aware that as you begin to see things as they are, it can be an uncomfortable experience. As is human nature, you may be tempted to flee back to your comfort zone.

Mindfulness won't insulate you from your life. In fact, it will do just the opposite. However, when you view the flow of your experiences with spaciousness, from the perspective that mindfulness allows, you're likely to find that there isn't anything to hide or escape from—that the flow of your life is just fine. Mindfulness isn't a quick fix or a miracle cure, designed to get rid of bad feelings or create a blissful panacea. It offers something more: the promise of accepting yourself and your experiences as they are and finding a richness that always exists within you and around you.

So above all, think of mindfulness as a way of responding to the events of your life, whatever they may be, and to yourself, with patience, openness, and compassion. Doing so will strengthen your deep and genuine connection with all those who share life with you, and even—perhaps especially—with yourself. To paraphrase Gandhi, it's a way of becoming the change you wish to see in the world.

By living mindfully, you'll usher in profound changes based on deep and heartfelt compassion. As you come to see your integral role in creation itself, your sense of separateness from the wonder and the flow of creation will fall away.

Patience, Openness, and Compassion

As you work with this book, you'll find that the more you create spacious mindful presence, the more the qualities of patience, openness, and compassion will naturally emerge. Although we're all familiar with the words "patience," "openness," and "compassion," they have some different shades of meaning in this book, so let's look at what I mean by each of them:

- **Patience** means allowing any given situation to evolve without imposing a need to manipulate, influence, or control the outcome. It means simply being with whatever is occurring, without fear-based, self-protective reactions. Patience is an invitation to wait for a mindful response to arise as you allow the flow of your experience to fully evolve without interrupting or distracting. Once your experience fully manifests, mindful responses often arise naturally.

- **Openness** means maintaining a sense of curiosity about the outcome of any experience. This is a curiosity unencumbered by opinions, prejudices, or expectations, an inquisitiveness in which you wonder how the situation is going to turn out. Openness also refers to opening your senses to the flow of experience and embracing the flow of your life as it occurs. This can bring a freshness to the way you're present amidst your experiences.

- **Compassion** means putting your need to manipulate and control outcomes aside and attuning to the needs and feelings of others—and your own needs and feelings. A genuinely compassionate attitude doesn't change in reaction to any given person or experience. It doesn't matter whether the other person is a close friend or an enemy—or even a person. Genuine compassion is about deep, heartfelt concern for the well-being of every living being in the universe. Compassion emerges as you maintain a spacious sense of patience and openness and hold your experiences with tenderness. This spaciousness opens the door to a greater resonance with all beings and allows you to respond more gently to the events and people around you—and to yourself.

The Importance of Trust

As you move through *The Mindfulness Workbook*, trust that the more you cultivate spaciousness, the more you will develop an awareness that generates genuine patience, openness, and compassion. The potential for careful, mindful responses is always present. These responses only need spaciousness and awareness in order to emerge. In fact, you're more likely to run into trouble when you think you know what to do. When you impose your thinking on your experiences, you can create alarm where no threat exists. As a result, you may close down and get stuck in fear-based thoughts, feelings, and actions. But when you cultivate clarity of awareness, you create reliable and careful responses. Unfortunately, how these emerge from the depths of your being cannot be described for you; you must experience it for yourself. Trust that this will happen as you remain patient and open to whatever occurs without imposing your fears and desires on events. Like every human, you are a naturally mindful being. Trust that as you clear away the obstructions, you will experience exactly what this means for you.

IS A FORMAL SITTING PRACTICE NECESSARY?

As to the question of whether a formal sitting practice is necessary, the answer is yes and no. In many respects, a formal seated practice of contemplative meditation is very valuable, offering a foundation for deepening your mindful responses in more and more areas of your life. Sitting practice takes many forms, all of them valuable, including Zen meditation, or *zazen*, which involves harmonizing the body, breathing, and mind to realize one's Buddha nature; *vipassana*, or insight meditation, which involves examining the nature of reality, including thought processes; contemplative meditation, which is similar to vipassana and may involve focusing on a certain aspect of reality or the nature of one's experience; and centering prayer, a method of contemplative prayer that emphasizes internal silence (Keating 1996). A major benefit of a formal seated practice is that it gives you time, on a daily basis, to be face to face with big deal mind, which is the source of so much suffering. I have maintained a formal seated practice for over thirty years, and it provides an invaluable foundation for moving into each day with spaciousness and mindful responsiveness.

That said, I also recognize that not everyone is interested in this sort of practice. If this is the case for you, you can still benefit from learning how to develop and maintain a dynamic practice of mindfulness that isn't as formalized. Since *The Mindfulness Workbook* is about a way of being in the world, the practices in this book will help you develop mindful living and integrate mindfulness into all aspects of your life without necessarily engaging in formal practice. However, the greatest benefits will come when you're able to move from a formal sitting practice to the vicissitudes of daily life while maintaining the spacious presence of your seated practice, with its qualities of patience, openness, and compassion.

BENEFITS OF MINDFULNESS

As you work with this book, you'll find that practicing mindful living will enhance the quality, richness, and depth of your life in many and meaningful ways. Mindful living can also enhance the effectiveness of both medical and psychological or emotional treatments, as evidenced by a growing body of research (Astin 1997; Brown and Ryan 2003; Kabat-Zinn et al. 1992, 1998).

The word "mindful" can be misleading, as it may be taken to mean that the experience is limited to a mental event or state. However, the research on mindfulness makes it abundantly clear that mindful responses involve the entire mind-body system. As you'll learn in chapter 1, the fear reaction that gives rise to mindlessness is a mind-body phenomenon, in both its origins and its effects. Developing spaciousness and mindfulness involves and affects the entire mind-body system, as well. Creating careful, mindful responses isn't merely an emotional, psychological event. Its benefits extend to the entire body and support healing and well-being on all levels.

COUNSELING AND MEDICATIONS

Although the benefits of mindfulness are impressive, I want to emphasize that there is no short-cut through suffering and no painless way around it. If you're dealing with thoughts, feelings, or behaviors that arise from long-standing difficulties or trauma, professional therapy will probably be necessary to help you along your healing journey. Incorporating mindful living practices will certainly enhance your healing, and you may wish to seek out a therapist who incorporates mindfulness practices into his or her practice.

Finally, if you are taking medications, don't make any adjustments to them without first consulting your health care professional. Clients and participants in workshops frequently ask me if mindful living will reduce or eliminate their need for medications. While this is certainly possible, it's important to proceed with caution and work closely with your therapist and health care professionals to determine whether this is the case for you.

HOW TO USE THE PRACTICES

The practices in this book are designed to be used repeatedly. While you may experience immediate benefits from a single practice, it's necessary to practice repeatedly if you are to attain long-term, lasting results. Gaining confidence in creating spacious presence and responding mindfully is a process. Feel free to make copies of each practice (for yourself only, please) and gather them in a folder or notebook so that you can easily return to them again and again. If you like, you can download an audio version of each of the practices in this book. Being guided in this way will enhance the experience. If this appeals to you, go to www.innerchg.com and click on the Download tab, then choose *The Mindfulness Workbook* to begin your download.

This chapter will outline several key elements that have a direct bearing on encouraging mindfulness in relationships: setting aside the "me versus you" distinctions of solid self; recognizing and resisting the various protective strategies you employ to protect your solid self; and specific techniques for cultivating patience, openness, and compassion in your relationships.

Foundations of Mindlessness and Mindfulness

Part 1 of this book will give you a background in mindlessness and mindfulness, along with an exploration of how each arises, then move on to creating a foundation for mindful living. Chapter 1 looks at the origins of mindlessness in fear-based reactions and how this creates suffering. Chapter 2 outlines how to create spacious presence amidst the unfolding of your life, allowing you to expand the practices in this book to inform your way of being in the world. Chapter 3 focuses on awareness of the breath and body. These are wonderful objects for mindfulness, as they're always present, everywhere you go. Mindful breathing and intentional relaxation can go a long way toward calming fear-based reactions and creating the spacious presence that invites you to hold all of your experiences with patience, openness, and compassion.

It's important to recognize that the goal of your work with mindfulness, both in this book and in your life, isn't to avoid having particular thoughts, feelings, reactions, opinions, distractions, or attachments. Not only are such challenges inevitable, they're actually the grist for the mindfulness mill. Every practice you work with is about learning to create the spacious presence that will help limit your need to react. This opens the door to responding to your life more deeply and with greater compassion and tenderness.

CHAPTER 1

Fear and Mindlessness

To fully understand the terrain of mindfulness, it's worthwhile to first explore the land of mindlessness. It is all too human to develop an array of habitual techniques and strategies that promote mindlessness and ultimately lead to suffering. By understanding the roots of your own mindlessness, you can start to recognize when you're falling into these patterns. This will also give you a clearer idea of how to achieve and maintain spacious mindful presence in all areas of your life. The first step is understanding that the origin of mindlessness is fear-based reactions to threats both actual and perceived, so looking at fear is where you must begin.

FEAR: THE BASIS OF MINDLESS REACTIONS

Before you read any further, simply accept that fear will influence you to resist your efforts to create spacious, mindful presence. Some fear is inevitable, and it's very powerful. It can become such a natural part of your daily experience that it's like breathing—something you do without being conscious or aware of it. If you don't recognize how your fears lead to mindlessness, you'll tend to look to events, others, and your past and future for explanations of your suffering, which can lead to a great deal of blaming, compensating, controlling, manipulating, and avoiding.

To develop mindful responses, you must equip yourself to recognize and deal with fear and anything else that interferes with mindful living. You can't impose a mindful mind-set on top of a mindless mind-set. Attempting to develop mindful living skills without first learning how to be present to and aware of mindless reactions is akin to trying to build a snowman in Costa Rica. Even if you get the snow there, you'll find that certain influences ultimately sabotage your efforts. Understanding these factors will allow you to better adapt to the conditions in your life. And perhaps you'll even discover that building a snowman wasn't what you really wanted in the first place!

There's an inflexibility in mindless living that arises from trying to force your fear-based coping strategies on your life, regardless of the outcome. You may have resorted to anger or anxiety, turned to divorce, or racked up a long list of physical symptoms. You may have tried endless diets, medications, or consumerism to "fix" your life, and then wondered why nothing is working. However, as long as your reactions are based in fear, very little will work. Pioneering psychologist Abraham Maslow (1966) said that if you have only a hammer in your toolbox, you end up reacting to everything as if it were a nail.

The Fight-or-Flight Reaction

Mindlessness isn't merely a concept; it has very real psychophysiological consequences that affect every aspect of your quality of life. Scientific inquiry into the mind-body connection has revealed that the mind and body function in unity and that disruption of any given aspect of the mind-body system has ramifications throughout. Medical anthropologist Dr. Walter Cannon introduced the concept of the fight-or-flight response to the medical literature in 1915. He demonstrated that any time an individual perceives danger or a threat in the environment, the same physiological response occurs: the *fight-or-flight response*, which prepares the mind-body system to protect itself from the perceived threat.

The fight-or-flight reaction is a hardwired response of the *autonomic nervous system* (ANS). The moment you perceive something that you interpret as a threat, your ANS registers this information and sends a flood of stress hormones into the body, directing your *sympathetic nervous system* (SNS) to prepare you to fight, flee, or freeze. One effect of this response is a narrowing of both cognitive mental functioning and behavioral responses. Your focus becomes narrowed so that you see only information related to the perceived threat. As a result, your subsequent behaviors are limited by your perception.

SYMPATHETIC NERVOUS SYSTEM

In its role as a watchdog on the lookout for any potential threats to your safety, the sympathetic nervous system exerts effects to keep your entire psychophysiology in a state of protective alert. Here are just a few of its actions:

- Increases heart rate and blood pressure

- Increases respiration

- Opens blood vessels to the heart

- Increases blood flow to the muscles by as much as 1,200 percent

- Releases adrenaline and other stress hormones

- Releases stored energy

- Dilates the pupils for improved visual scanning of the environment for threats

- Increases sweating

- Reduces blood flow to the skin

All these physiological reactions also affect your cognitive function. For example, stress hormones such as adrenaline and cortisol narrow your cognitive focus to signals in your environment associated with the perceived threat. As a result, you continually perceive your environment as a danger, creating a feedback loop that can keep your SNS in a constant state of alert, which I refer to as a slow adrenaline drip. This interferes with activation of the *parasympathetic nervous system* (PNS), which normally helps moderate the effects of stress. A constant state of SNS arousal is known as *autonomic dysregulation*.

PARASYMPATHETIC NERVOUS SYSTEM

The parasympathetic nervous system is responsible for rest and healing throughout the body. Activation of this branch is what allows you to quiet down, rest, and fall asleep. If overactivation of the SNS prevents the PNS from moderating the fight-or-flight response, numerous physical symptoms arise: sleep disturbances, digestive disruptions, irritable bowel syndrome, anxiety or panic, depressed mood, irritability, headaches, respiratory distress, and more. Here are some of the most important functions of the parasympathetic nervous system:

- Decreases heart rate and blood pressure

- Slows breathing

- Lubricates the mouth and eyes

- Turns on digestive function, allowing the body to store energy

- Constricts the pupils

- Allows elimination and reproductive functions to resume

- Stimulates the body's healing responses

- Allows for rest and sleep

Interestingly, when we experience a sense of space (going to the beach, the mountains, or other places where we can "get away from it all"), the PNS is activated and the body enters its rest and restorative mode, moderating the effects of stress.

Kindling and the Fear Reaction

Strangely enough, you need not even be threatened or stressed in order to experience activation of the SNS. It can be activated by thoughts and memories, as is abundantly evident in people who suffer from post-traumatic stress disorder. If a perceived threat makes a strong enough impression, either in a single intense incident or by being repeated over time, the body learns to activate the SNS any time another situation seems similar to that original threat. Repeated stimulation of the SNS, whether by external threats or internal stimuli, is referred to as *kindling*. With repeated exposure to the same fear stimuli, the fear response is kindled increasingly easily, so that eventually it can occur in the complete absence of threatening stimuli (Post et al. 1998).

In humans, the threat doesn't have to be real; it only needs to be perceived as real. For example, hearing the screeching of tires, anticipating the talk you plan to have with your boss about a raise, or arguing with your son about his curfew can all be perceived as threatening. The body responds to these perceived psychological threats just as it would to real physical threats, and your entire psychophysiology closes down in a protective mode where there is no room for spaciousness and mindful responses. You begin to feel yourself as separate from yourself and from the experience you're having. Your physical being constricts as your muscles tighten, your thoughts race, your heart rate increases, and your breathing becomes rapid and shallow. I refer to this as a state of *solid self*. In this mode, you will act to protect a sense of identity you've become attached to, rather than responding to events around you flexibly and mindfully.

On the other hand, when the ANS is functioning in a balanced fashion, with normal fluctuation between the SNS and PNS, immune function improves, interactions between the heart and brain improve, brain wave activity relaxes, learning and memory are enhanced, and digestion improves. This is the state that allows open, patient, and compassionate responses—mindful responses—to emerge.

The Shift

Developing spaciousness is at the core of the mind-body shift from SNS activity to PNS activity. When you learn how to be in the presence of the experiences of your life without becoming caught up in your fear-based protective reactions, you have opened the door to mindful living. The practices in this book will help you experience and become aware of this shift from SNS activity to the more patient, open, and compassionate space facilitated by PNS activity. The entire mind-body system is affected by this shift that moves from reacting to responding, from fear to acceptance, from restriction to openness, and from mistrust to trust.

Big Deal Mind

I think of the state of mind that arises under the influence of the SNS as *big deal mind*. Because it manifests in so many ways, I'll use a variety of terms to refer to it throughout this book, including fear mind, reactive mind, illusion mind, delusion mind, and aggression mind. This is to avoid solidifying big deal mind as a monumental or specific concept; instead, I want to reinforce the idea that big deal mind is the process you use to resist the unpredictable in your life. Big deal mind draws your energy into a stream of minor details and reacts as if these things are important. It responds to your fear by latching onto specific experiences in your life and making a big deal out of them, rather than seeing them as isolated incidents in the ongoing flow of your life. The mantra of big deal mind is "Here, pay attention to this instead," drawing your attention away from a meaningful connection with the spacious quality of your life and narrowing your focus to fear-based preoccupations. Big deal mind focuses on aspects of your experience related to fear reactions and then spins out a stream of related big deals associated with whatever you fear at the moment.

Let's take a moment to reflect on how the struggle with big deal mind has been depicted in Christianity and Buddhism. When Jesus ventured into the desert for forty days and forty nights to confront temptation, he had to deal with the Devil (a manifestation of big deal mind) in his lair. When the Devil boasted that he owned the world, Jesus didn't argue, nor did he overwhelm the Devil with majestic splendor; he simply held his ground until the Devil went away. Similarly, the Buddha decided to give up his various spiritual quests and sit beneath the Bodhi tree, vowing to steadfastly remain until he vanquished the veils of suffering. Just as Jesus was challenged by the Devil, Buddha faced the demon temptress Mara, who threw various enticements at him in an attempt to seduce him back into the world of suffering. Mara retreated only when she realized that Buddha wouldn't react to her efforts, at which point he attained enlightenment.

Both of these stories reflect the role big deal mind plays in its efforts to get you to "pay attention to this instead." Notice how Jesus and Buddha both willingly sat with and experienced their fear-based demons. You must venture into that territory and know it for what it is in order to reap the full benefits of mindfulness. Notice also that Jesus and Buddha each utilized non-reactive spacious presence to defeat their foes. From this stance, you can see that neither you nor your experience is defined by your fears, and that you need not buy into those fears or even react to them.

Consider the scene in the movie *The Wizard of Oz* when Dorothy and her entourage arrive at the Emerald City and are in the terrifying presence of the Great Oz, a disembodied head with a booming voice. When Toto runs over and pulls back a curtain, he exposes an elderly man frantically speaking into a microphone and operating the dials and levers that create the illusion of the Great Oz. Thus exposed, he yells into the microphone, "Do not pay any attention to that man behind the curtain." This is exactly how big deal mind works, keeping you focused on the activity projected onto your awareness screen and insisting, "Pay attention to this instead!" Fear operates the dials of big deal mind and is bent on keeping you distracted.

The next time you're near a newsstand, take some time to peruse the magazine covers and read blurbs for the lead articles. You'll probably find that many of them are designed to elicit fear: you aren't thin enough, you need plastic surgery, your stomach muscles aren't ripped enough, you aren't managing your life or relationships well, the food you eat is killing you, aliens are going to invade Earth—you get the idea. All too often, media messages generate self-doubt and insecurity. When you take these messages at face value and operate from a place of fear, you'll find it difficult to embrace your authentic self. Remember, fear isn't always about external threats to your safety; it can also be fear of loss, fear of change, fear of meeting new people, fear of failure, and an endless array of threatening internal material.

Big deal mind endeavors to protect your sense of a fixed identity—your solid self—in a variety of ways, particularly by obscuring your consciousness with the veils of illusion, delusion, attachment, and aggression, which I'll discuss at length in chapters 4 through 7. By attempting to protect and preserve your solid self, these strategies result in a resistance to the flow of life and ultimately lead to suffering. The practices in this book will help you learn how to be in the presence of these strategies without getting caught up in fear-based reactions. In many of the practices, I'll ask you to pay attention to how your body feels. As you learn to notice the shift from SNS to PNS functioning, you'll come to see how that relates to the emergence of more mindful responses, and as you learn to respond rather than react, the influence of your fear will steadily diminish.

THE MINDFULNESS ATTITUDE

Before you try the first practice, let's take a look at how to assume an attitude of mindfulness. The following four easy steps will create spacious receptivity within your mind and body simultaneously:

1. Drop your shoulders, allowing gravity to bring them down to a comfortable and restful position.

2. Loosen your jaw. Again, just let gravity bring your jaw to a comfortable and restful position.

3. Soften your gaze. I often verbalize this as "seeing without looking." Just see whatever is in your visual field without looking *at* anything. In some of the practices, such as the one that follows, I'll ask you to close your eyes and visualize. Softening your gaze applies when your eyes are shut, as well as when they're open.

4. Take several nice, easy, deep breaths, and rest in this space for few minutes.

❧ PRACTICE: Observing Big Deal Mind ❧

This first practice is designed to help you consciously experience your big deal mind and simply watch how it operates, a process I sometimes refer to as *clear seeing*. In chapter 2 we'll return to this practice and develop it further.

As for all of the practices in this book, first read through the instructions until you're familiar with them, then put the book down and focus on doing the practice. (You may also download an audio version of all of the practices in the book at www.innerchg.com.) Unless instructed otherwise, practice in a place that's quiet and where you won't be disturbed. A seated position is generally best, so you can be comfortable but not so relaxed that you might fall asleep.

Adopt the attitude of mindfulness, closing your eyes and resting comfortably for a few minutes. Let all of your muscles relax—in your shoulders, face, jaw, neck, stomach, hands, and legs, let them all relax.

Once you're relaxed, imagine yourself sitting in a movie theater. This is your own private theater; it's safe and no one else is in it. You're sitting several rows back from the screen, and it's comfortably dark. Up on the screen you begin to see the thoughts, emotions, memories, and sensations that pass through your awareness.

Just sit and watch. Don't follow any particular thought or emotion into the screen, just as you wouldn't try to jump into the screen during a movie. Just watch without judgment, reaction, or distraction. You are here simply to become familiar with how big deal mind functions; you don't have to do anything about it during this practice.

As you observe your big deal mind, simply take note of what it presents; for example, "Oh, there's my credit card thought... There's a thought about being frustrated with my spouse or partner... There's the thought 'This is really boring'... There's self-doubt... There's the thought 'I've got so much paperwork to do'... There's the thought 'My mother-in-law is coming to visit'... There's the thought 'I'm not doing this right'..."

Sit comfortably and watch as the stream of thoughts flows past, not following any thought in particular. Notice which thoughts have a pull on your attention and emotions—which thoughts start to draw you into what's on the screen. Becoming lost in particular thoughts or drawn into your mental drama means you've fallen under the influence of big deal mind. Also note any physical sensations you experience.

If you find that you've been drawn into a thought, feeling, memory, or other experience that big deal mind offered, simply return to your seat and return to watching without involvement or attachment.

Stay with this for a few minutes, then open your eyes and take some time to contemplate and answer the following questions.

What was it like to simply watch the succession of thoughts, emotions, and sensations that routinely clutter your awareness and experience?

_____

_____

_____

_____

Which thoughts, feelings, and sensations created the greatest emotional reaction?

_____

_____

_____

_____

What physical reactions did you notice? (For example, pain, a pounding heart, muscle tension, tingling, nausea, or headache.) Which thoughts and emotions created the greatest physical reaction?

_____

_____

_____

_____

As you simply watched how your big deal mind works, what was it like to not be drawn into the screen?

_____

_____

_____

_____

As you simply watched how your big deal mind functions, did you learn anything about the ways you maintain your suffering? What did you learn?

_____

_____

_____

_____

_____

Make note of these physical reactions and learn to use them as cues to your internal state. When you notice similar physical reactions in the future, be aware that this could be an indicator that big deal mind is reacting to a perceived physical or psychological threat. Troublesome as they may seem to be, reactions such as anxiety, tension, fear, judgments, the need to be right, and so on are the very tools you will use to become aware of and minimize mindless reactions. When you sense these reactions occurring, pause for a moment and practice this theater experience to access your clear seeing and make room for responses that emanate from a deep place of patience, openness, and compassion.

SOLID SELF

As mentioned earlier, SNS fear-based reactions produce a sense of being physically and emotionally separate from the flow of your life. Your muscles tighten, your heart rate increases, your breathing becomes rapid, your hair stands on end, and your arteries constrict to prepare you to react to whatever threat you perceive. In this state, you feel that your survival depends upon protecting your solid self from harm.

What is solid self? It's the sense that there's a permanent "you" that remains essentially fixed and unchanging through space and time. In Western psychology, this is often referred to as the personality. From a place of mindfulness—awareness of and attention to the ongoing experiences of your life—there is no such thing. Although the differences may be subtle, the you of today is not the you of yesterday, and it certainly isn't the you of ten, twenty, or thirty years ago. As a marriage and family therapist, I frequently hear laments along the lines of "He isn't the man I married!" While this may be distressing, it's also inevitable. Human beings aren't impervious to the processes of change that affect all living beings. When you're attached to solid self, to a permanent, unchanging "you," you must continually protect that self and prevent any redefinition, no matter what the circumstances. As you can imagine, attachment to an identity that doesn't fit the current situation can be the source of great suffering.

Here's an example: When Bill arrives home from work and walks through the door, his wife asks, "Did you pick up the dry cleaning? I need that dress for the awards banquet tonight." He forgot. On the way home he was immersed in his solid sense of self. He was thinking about the awards banquet and going over his acceptance speech in his mind. He was caught up in thoughts about how proud his wife will be of him and how the award will improve his standing in the community. Becoming overinvolved in his solid self, Bill was disconnected from his awareness of what was needed. Now when the actual events of his life (his wife's request that he pick up her dress) confront him, his surprise activates his SNS as he feels his solid self under attack. His big deal mind moves in to protect the image he was immersed in during his drive home. He also perceives his wife as a solid self, and as a threat. Rather than responding by acknowledging his oversight and trying to come up with a solution, he reacts angrily, saying, "I can't believe you asked me to do that, on this of all days!" And so the suffering begins.

As you can see, attachment to an identity that doesn't fit the current situation can be the source of great suffering as attempts to freeze your sense of self in space and time create a self-centered isolation. Preservation of the solid self requires acting upon your experiences as though they're separate from you. However, solid self is nothing more than the accumulation of conditioned reactions, opinions, and desires that clog up the flow of your life. As these messages of how you're supposed to think and feel disconnect you from how your experience is actually unfolding, you can be torn apart by the conflict between what's actually occurring and what you wish were occurring.

✑ PRACTICE: Listening to Your Body ✑

This practice offers you the opportunity to become sensitive to the way your body reinforces your experience of solid self. This is a two-part practice. The first part involves observing your reactions to a situation that you envision and experience mentally. In the second part, you'll observe your reactions to a real-life situation.

Adopt the attitude of mindfulness, closing your eyes and resting comfortably for a few minutes. Let all of your muscles relax—in your shoulders, face, jaw, neck, stomach, hands, and legs, let them all relax.

Now bring a recent stressful experience into your awareness. Choose something that's currently causing you distress and suffering but not something traumatic. Take your time and envision all aspects of this situation: where you are, who is there, what is being said, and what is being done. Bring to awareness as many aspects of this experience as possible, such as the time of day, and information from all of your senses. Stay immersed in this experience for several minutes.

Keeping your eyes closed, begin to direct your awareness to your body. Begin at the top of your head and scan down over your face, neck, shoulders, arms, fingers, torso, hips, legs, and feet.

When you complete the scan, open your eyes and take some time to contemplate and answer the following questions.

How did your body feel while you were immersed in this difficult remembered experience? How did your jaw, neck, and shoulders feel? How about other areas? Describe in detail what happened to your body during this practice.

_____

_____

_____

_____

_____

With the awareness that the way your body tightens up is an attempt to ward off actual or perceived threats and preserve the solid self, what did you learn about how stressful experiences affect or activate this system?

_____

_____

_____

_____

Did other people or other parts of your remembered experience seem to present a threat to your sense of self? What did you observe about your attempts to protect your solid self through physical reactions and how this contributes to keeping other people or other parts of your experience solid and separate from you?

_____

_____

_____

_____

_____

The second part of this practice invites you to bring this same awareness to a similar experience as it happens, such as an argument with a coworker, a partner, or a child, getting a notice that you forgot to pay a bill and are being charged a late fee, or sitting in traffic when you're in a hurry. As soon as possible after this real-life experience, take the time to answer the same questions.

How did your body feel while you were immersed in this difficult experience? How did your jaw, neck, and shoulders feel? How about other areas? Describe in detail what happened to your body during this practice.

_____

_____

_____

_____

_____

With the awareness that the way your body tightens up is an attempt to ward off actual or perceived threats and preserve the solid self, what did you learn about how stressful experiences affect or activate this system?

_____

_____

_____

_____

Did other people or other parts of your experience seem to present a threat to your sense of self? What did you observe about your attempts to protect your solid self through physical reactions and how this contributes to keeping other people or other parts of your experience solid and separate from you?

_____

_____

_____

_____

From now on, any time you feel these same physical responses, take a moment to check in and see whether this is due to a fear-based reaction and attempts to protect the solid self. Likewise, when you feel a sense of disconnection from others, look at whether big deal mind is playing a role in your reactions. The physical sensations that signal emergence of your solid self can be a powerful tool to keep you connected to your experiences and help you develop an expanding spacious presence. Rather than feeling at the mercy of fears and physical tension, you can use these experiences to further your growth in mindfulness. In this way, your antagonist can become your teacher.

SUMMARY

Fear is the root cause of mindless living. When your mode of living is characterized by fear-based reactions, you'll find yourself disconnected from the actual flow of your experiences, from others, and from your own thoughts and feelings. The practices in this chapter have helped you become familiar with your big deal mind and some of the clues that it's in control, causing you to react rather than respond. Now that you're equipped with this awareness, the next chapter will help you explore how creating and maintaining spacious presence will decrease the tendency to fall into fear-based, mindless reactions and, as a result, decrease your suffering.

CHAPTER 2

Spaciousness, Compassion, and Mindfulness

Now that we've spent some time looking at mindlessness and its origins in fear, you're probably wondering how you can can make the shift to mindfulness. I find the teachings of Mexican shaman Miguel Ruiz (1997) and Jesuit priest and psychotherapist Anthony DeMello (1990) useful in this regard. Both explore the notion of being in a type of dream state that disconnects you from truly experiencing the richness of your life and the depth of your true nature. They encourage awakening from this dream to fully and compassionately embrace yourself and your life and all of the richness and depth inherent in your experiences. Waking up requires that you unlearn the habits of thought and behavior that cause your suffering and let go of resistance to what occurs.

As you now know, activation of big deal mind is typically a process of closing down that disconnects you from the flow of your life, from others, and from your authentic self. In this chapter, you'll experience how you can be in the presence of big deal mind without closing down. You will discover how to be amidst your thoughts, feelings, and memories with a profound sense of spaciousness, holding your experiences with patience, openness, and compassion. As you become more skillful in maintaining a lasting spaciousness, mindful responses will arise.

Don't expect the practices in this chapter—and in the book as a whole—to yield specific or desired outcomes. This sort of attachment to outcome feeds big deal mind with another big deal to pay attention to. This can even extend to identifying with the practice itself: "Hey! Look at me, I practice mindfulness."

SPACIOUSNESS FIRST, THEN MINDFULNESS

Many years ago, I attended a rodeo in Cody, Wyoming. When the rodeo was over, I stood in the bleachers and watched as the horses and bulls were released into a pasture behind the arena. There was quite an uproar as the animals made use of their freedom and spacious surrounds. They kicked up their heels, snorted, and rolled around, stirring up a huge cloud of dust, but after a while they all began to settle down. Some laid down to rest, others grazed, and others drank out of the trough. A sense of peace and quiet emerged from all of that riotous activity.

Creating spaciousness is akin to what I witnessed that evening. If you open the gate and invite spaciousness to emerge, a profound sense of calm will arise from the formerly riotous activity of big deal mind. Developing this calm spaciousness is at the very heart of mindful responses. Spaciousness isn't a difficult concept; it's something that some part of you knows very well. In many ways, we seek space in our lives. When we go on vacation, many of us gravitate toward wide-open spaces, where we can get some breathing room: the mountains, the beach, the forest. We intuitively know the benefits of spaciousness for our health and well-being. As you work with the practices in this book, you'll learn how to create spaciousness; this will lead to profound changes in your very being, which will radiate outward and affect all aspects of your life.

It Isn't About the Salt

Here's a wonderful allegory about spaciousness: If you were to dissolve a tablespoon of salt in a small glass of water and then drink it, what would your reaction be? The flavor of the salt would be overwhelming, and you'd probably reject the glass of water as unpleasant. But what if you take that same tablespoon of salt and dissolve it in a vast, clean lake, then dip a glass in and drink it? Where's the salt? Where's the unpleasantness?

Clearly the problem isn't the salt; it's the size of the container. Think of the conditioned thoughts, feelings, and actions that contribute to your suffering as being similar. The smaller the container, the greater your experience of suffering. Look at the container of your life and realize that developing spaciousness will allow you to expand this container, broadening your focus, and your experience, so that suffering is only one element of the richness all around you.

Clear Seeing

Clear seeing is pivotal to many of the concepts and practices you'll encounter in this book. Clear seeing isn't an esoteric, mystical concept; it's simply watching what's occurring, not just in your external environment, but also in your thoughts and feelings and other aspects of your internal world. Clear seeing doesn't involve figuring things out, analyzing, or judging what's occurring. It involves watching who you are and being aware of the newness inherent in every moment and every experience. It's also characterized by a sense of wonder and curiosity that adds a sense of lightness to your life.

You've already started to access clear seeing with the theater practice in chapter 1. As you continue to develop clear seeing in the practices throughout this book, you'll find that it helps you see through the distractions and strategies of big deal mind. In fact, bringing clear seeing, with its sense of wonder and curiosity, to reactivity and protective strategies can help remove the seriousness often associated with mindfulness. As you look into the workings of big deal mind, try to keep it light, operating from a stance of "Gee, I wonder what's happening now. Where is big deal mind going, and what is it trying to get me to focus on?" This simple process of watching keeps you from jumping into the screen to become involved in whatever drama big deal mind presents. With clear seeing, you'll be able to notice when and how big deal mind surfaces and how you can resist its seduction. With time, clear seeing may even prevent activation of reactive mind, or at least keep its activity to a minimum.

When reactive mind quiets down, you can let go of the concepts, opinions, and preformulated ideas you carry around and begin to see the beauty of the life that is continually unfolding in and around you. By observing yourself, your life, and the world around you with patience, openness, and compassion, you can come to recognize how mindlessness causes your suffering. With clear seeing, you become increasingly attentive to your experience on all levels, and this goes a long way in creating the spaciousness necessary to engage in heartfelt and careful gestures, even in the smallest of actions.

Clear seeing is also referred to as "beginner's mind," a mind that's innocent of preconceptions, judgments, and prejudices, allowing you to be present to explore and observe things as they are. Think of it like the mind of a small child, full of curiosity and wonder. Beginner's mind isn't already made up—it remains playful and curious.

To Be Mindful Is to Be Careful

A distant synonym of the word "mindful" is "careful," which underscores the importance of embracing mindfulness as a response, rather than viewing it as a mind-set. Mindfulness means allowing careful, compassionate responses to develop in response to the flow of your life experiences. As you practice and explore spaciousness, you'll come to see how it creates the opening for careful and mindful responses to emerge.

PRESENT AMIDST THE NOISE

As you begin to explore mindful living, the best place to start is by looking openly, patiently, and compassionately at yourself. You must be present with yourself if you are to be present in your life. The practices in this chapter will help you be present with your thoughts, feelings, reactions, attachments, and demands, your strengths and weaknesses, and your successes and failures without resorting to fear-based reactions. This requires courage—and just to be clear, courage isn't the absence of fear, it's persistence in the face of fear. As you work with the practices in this chapter, you'll discover where your attention and energy are going, how this affects your health and well-being, and how you can develop greater spaciousness.

I recently went to a talk given by a Zen master. The audience was made up of people who were new to the experience of mindfulness. He was discussing what mindfulness is and how to bring mindful living into daily life. He guided the audience through a mindful practice that lasted about twenty-five minutes. Afterward, a man raised his hand and said, "My mind was always busy. There was the constant noise of thinking. I thought mindfulness was supposed to get you to be quieter and stop all that noisy thinking." The master replied, "Mindfulness helps you just be present amidst the noise." Through the practices in this book, you'll learn that spaciousness is what allows you to maintain your presence amidst the noise. Learning to maintain this spaciousness as your life unfolds, no matter what the circumstances, will bring you a long way toward living mindfully.

❧ PRACTICE: Glimpsing Spacious Presence ❧

The first half of this practice is the same as the first practice in the book, but the second half will enter new territory, giving you a glimpse of how you can be in the presence of big deal mind without getting caught up in fear-based reactions. This glimpse will help you see the actual flow of your life with greater depth and clarity. As a result, you'll be able to see the ineffectiveness of typical strategies (illusion, delusion, attachment, and aggression), and with each glimpse, they will lose their influence. Your glimpse may be fleeting; it may last a few seconds, or it may last several minutes. The length of time isn't important. What is important is noticing the impact this glimpse has on your entire mind-body system. Notice how you feel the shift from SNS to PNS functioning and how this shift invites deeper and more meaningful mindful responses.

Before you enter this practice, take a moment to check in with your expectations regarding the outcome. Let go of any expectations and instead be open to whatever occurs.

Adopt the attitude of mindfulness, closing your eyes and resting comfortably for a few minutes. Let all of your muscles relax—in your shoulders, face, jaw, neck, stomach, hands, and legs, let them all relax.

Once you're relaxed, imagine yourself sitting in a movie theater. As before, this is your own private theater; it's safe and no one else is in it. You're sitting several rows back from the screen, and it's comfortably dark. Up on the screen you begin to see the thoughts, emotions, memories, and sensations that pass through your awareness.

Just sit and watch. Don't follow any particular thought or emotion into the screen, just as you wouldn't try to jump into the screen during a movie. Just watch without judgment, reaction, or distraction.

As you observe your big deal mind, simply take note of what it presents; simply watch and name. Notice which thoughts have a pull on your attention and emotions, and also note any physical sensations you experience. Stay with this for a few minutes before moving on to the next part of the practice.

Now imagine that there's another "you" in this theater, sitting all the way in the back of the theater, in the very last row directly behind the first you. This second you is just sitting there watching the you up front, who is still just watching the screen.

Stay with this for a few minutes and notice what happens, paying particular attention to your emotional, physical, and mental reactions.

Now imagine that there is a third you, standing back by the door of the theater. This third you is simply watching the second you, seated in the back row of the theater, who is still watching the you in the front, who is still watching all that is passing across the screen.

Stay with this for a few minutes, then open your eyes and take some time to contemplate and answer the following questions.

What was it like to be the first you, watching the succession of thoughts, emotions, and sensations on the screen of your awareness?

_____

_____

_____

_____

Which thoughts, feelings, and sensations created the greatest emotional reaction?

_____

_____

_____

_____

What physical reactions did you notice? (For example, pain, a pounding heart, muscle tension, tingling, nausea, or headache.) Which thoughts and emotions created the greatest physical reaction?

_____

_____

_____

_____

What did you notice, emotionally and physically, when you were the second you?

_____

_____

_____

_____

What did you notice, emotionally and physically, when you were the third you?

_____

_____

_____

_____

As you became the second you and then the third you, what was it like to experience being in the presence of your big deal mind and not be drawn into the screen?

_____

_____

_____

_____

As you were the second you and the third you, did you get a glimpse of the shift to a more mindful state, a shift from SNS to PNS functioning? How did this shift occur for you?

_____

_____

_____

_____

_____

Continue working with this practice. Try it again, perhaps when you're actually in the throes of big deal mind; you might be ruminating over a conflict with your partner, worrying about something you heard on television, or feeling fearful about your health or the health of a loved one. Perhaps visualizing is difficult for you. If this is the case, don't worry. This book includes a wide variety of practices that help create spaciousness, and many of them don't require visualizing. Different approaches work better for different people. This is one reason why I've included so many practices in this book.

No matter what the outcome of this particular practice, realize that this is just one step in a lifelong process of becoming familiar with how your solid self and big deal mind can lead you down a path toward mindlessness and suffering. There is no need to judge or criticize yourself or that process, and no need to try to stop it. Just watch it with openness, patience, and compassion. Remember, the first step in living more mindfully is to look within and start to understand what makes you tick without turning it into something to judge yourself about. The sense of spaciousness you may have glimpsed in this practice will help you be in the presence of your thoughts, emotions, and sensations without getting caught up in them or identifying with them. As you begin to see yourself beyond your content, you'll develop a greater and deeper sense of your true self—a self that is an integral part of the vast miracle and beauty of life.

Mary's Story

Mary, a forty-two-year-old human-resources manager who is married with three children, came in to see me describing a great deal of anxiety and anger over her mother-in-law's visits. Even just mention of visits or planning for them elicited a great deal of agitation. She described her mother-in-law, Eunice, as mean-spirited, controlling, critical, and self-centered. She also reported that Eunice had suddenly lost her husband in an accident with a drunk driver several years back.

Whenever an impending visit approached, Mary started having more conflicts with her husband, had difficulty sleeping, and often got headaches. She also tended to overeat. "I have to learn to get over this!" Mary protested. "It's ridiculous that she has so much control over me!"

As Mary talked, I noticed that the muscles in her neck were very tense, her breathing was rapid and shallow, and her speech was rushed—all signs of SNS activity. Even though her mother-in-law was nowhere near at the time, Mary's experience was dominated by her mother-in-law and everything she conjured up for Mary.

I guided Mary through the preceding practice, of being in a theater and then shifting her perspective to a second self and then a third self, and then asked her to simply allow the image of her mother-in-law to come onto the screen. As Mary sat with that image, then shifted to the second and then the third Mary, she began reporting a shift in her experience.

"Oh my God!" she whispered. "Two things happened. I can now see my own fear and what a scared little girl is sitting up in the front of the theater. I feel such compassion for her! And as I'm standing in the back of the theater as the third me, I can really see how my mother-in-law's behaviors are coming from such a deep place of pain for her. She looks so sad and lonely. I think being a widow has been just awful for her."

Mary started crying. "That little girl in the front of the theater was so afraid of not being good enough; she didn't know how to react. Standing back here, I now have feelings of compassion for my mother-in-law and see that I need to be more patient and understanding of her pain." By the end of the session, Mary's breathing was more relaxed, her voice was softer, and the tension in her neck had visibly decreased. She also reported that her headache wasn't as bad as when she arrived at my office. All of these changes were evidence of her shift to PNS activity.

Mary continued to practice this at home, and after her mother-in-law's next visit she called me to say the visit had been much better than past ones. She said she had felt more even-keeled, and that she had often been able to respond to her mother-in-law with more patience and compassion.

᪬ PRACTICE: Letting the Mud Settle ᪬

Mindless living is perpetuated by keeping your focus continually stirred up. As Lao-tzu asked, "Do you have the patience to wait until your mud settles and the water is clear?" This practice explores that question, allowing you to learn the important skill of being in the presence of a concern and having the patience to let the mud settle and the water clear; to watch your sense of impatience and urgency without engaging in your fear reaction.

Assume the attitude of mindfulness. Take three slow breaths, breathing in through your nose and releasing the air through your mouth gently and easily. Let all of your muscles relax—in your shoulders, face, jaw, neck, stomach, hands, and legs, let them all relax. Rest here for several minutes.

Take a moment and let a concern come to mind. It can be a present concern, such as finances, a relationship struggle, a medical issue, difficulties in your career, a specific fear, or a struggle with anxiety or depression. It can also be a lingering concern from your past, such as loss of a loved one, issues with a parent, low self-worth, or a missed opportunity. However, please avoid choosing an issue related to a significant trauma, such as violence, abuse, or abandonment, especially the first few times you do this practice. As you work with this practice over time, you may be able to use it with more serious concerns, perhaps with the support of a therapist.

Rest in the presence of this concern. Just watch it without judgment, reaction, or distraction.

Using your imagination, allow an image symbolizing your concern to come into your awareness. It may arrive in your awareness as a color, a shape, an animal, a person, a substance (anything from sand to water to Jell-O), or an object (such as a book, a leaf, a rolling pin), or just about anything you can imagine. Avoid censoring this image. Be open and patient. If it doesn't come right away, that's alright; just take your time.

Once you have that image in mind, visualize yourself standing in front of a table. On that table is a large, crystal clear bowl filled three-quarters full with a clear liquid. (Notice that I don't indicate what sort of liquid; let your imagination define this.) Next to this bowl is a spoon.

Recall your symbolic representation of your concern, then place it into the bowl and start stirring.

Keep stirring for at least two minutes and observe what happens as you stir.

Stop stirring and put the spoon down, then step back and observe what happens. After observing for a minute or two, answer the following questions.

What happened to the symbolic representation of your concern when you placed it in the bowl?

_____

_____

_____

_____

_____

As you began stirring, what did you notice about your concern?

_____

_____

_____

_____

_____

As you kept stirring, what happened to your concern?

_____

_____

_____

_____

_____

As you kept stirring, what did you notice about how you felt, both emotionally and physically?

_____

_____

_____

_____

_____

When you stopped stirring, what happened to your concern?

_____

_____

_____

_____

_____

When you stopped stirring, how did you feel, both physically and emotionally? Did you notice a shift? If so what did you experience?

There is no right way to have this experience. Perhaps the water didn't clear when you quit stirring. It may have remained agitated, cloudy, muddy, or colored. That's fine. People often ask questions like "What does it mean if my symbol didn't dissolve?" "What if my symbol got bigger?" or "What if my water didn't clear?" That just means that your symbol didn't dissolve, that it got bigger, or that your water didn't clear. Remember, this is just a visualization—a way of conceiving of big deal mind. It doesn't predict any outcome in the real world.

However, there is a lesson here: When you stop letting your fear mind continually stir things up in your life, you'll begin to feel a shift. This practice allows you to experience that shift in a metaphorical way, through visualization. Everyone experiences this practice differently, and we each experience the shift in a unique way, as well. It isn't important to interpret the experience. Just watch what happens and see how the shift brings a new awareness into your life, allowing you to develop a new relationship to whatever your big deal was.

Jason's Story

Jason, twenty-three years old, came to see me for help with emotional issues related to a sports injury he suffered in high school. While playing football, he sustained a shoulder separation and required surgery to repair it. Although surgery did "fix" the injury, he continued to experience significant pain.

Jason had tried many things to get rid of his "@#$*%!" pain: physical therapy, acupuncture, medication, and more. Throughout his initial sessions with me, he routinely referred to his pain as something disconnected from his experience. He perceived his pain as something that was being done to him, and he wanted to get rid of it. His body language and his comments all reflected his resistance to his experience. I pointed out that doing battle with his pain was a factor in perpetuating his pain. If nothing else, keeping the affected muscles and nerves in a constant state of tension was interfering with his body's ability to heal.

He wasn't happy with this and asked, "So, what am I supposed to do? Just give in to the pain and let it take over?" I pointed out that doing battle with his pain had already taken over his life—that the major focus in his life was everything he had done or was doing to get rid of the pain.

When I guided him through the practice above, he symbolized his pain as a steel ball with spikes all over it. As he stirred, he noticed how much noise the ball made as it clanked around inside the bowl. He also noticed that if he stirred too hard, the ball might break the bowl, and then he'd have a real mess on his hands.

When he stopped stirring, the ball dropped to the bottom of the bowl and just sat there. I encouraged him to stay with that—being in the presence of the steel ball as it simply sat there. As he did this, his shoulder twitched and he let out a big sigh. Then he said, "Wow! It's like something in my shoulder just let go!"

When we finished the session, he commented, "I had no idea that doing so little could do so much!" While Jason's pain didn't disappear, he did experience a major reduction in the pain. He also reported that much of this reduction was due to not paying so much attention to his pain. At our last session, he said, "I've stopped fighting with it, and now I have more energy to focus on other things in my life."

EXPANDING YOUR OPTIONS

As Jason's story shows, the experience of letting your mud settle illuminates two important benefits of spaciousness and the shift to PNS functioning. First, it reveals how fear-based attempts to get rid of problems keep you stirred up as you try to reject and control your experiences. This interferes with the ability to explore different perspectives and approaches to problems. When you stop stirring things up and let the mud settle, you'll find a clarity that will allow you to see mindful solutions—solutions that were probably there all along but remained obscured. The second benefit is that when you stop stirring and allow yourself to maintain spacious presence, you can let go of reactions, judgments, and resistance to unwanted aspects of yourself and your experience. This allows you to be open to learning whatever your concerns have been trying to get you to pay attention to. Perhaps there's something important that you've been ignoring.

WATCHING THOUGHTS AND FEELINGS

Watching thoughts and feelings is a more traditional approach to creating mindfulness of your inner experiential life. It's an opportunity to say hello to your experiences, rather than trying to escape them. This approach can help you develop great patience in regard to whatever is occurring in the flow of your life. As you work on watching your thoughts and feelings in the next practice, you'll simply acknowledge troublesome thoughts and feelings rather than closing down around them with habitual fear-based reactions. This practice involves being in the presence of your experiences with a genuine curiosity and interest and embracing every moment, knowing that within each experience you'll find what you need for a mindful response to that experience. Before we enter the practice, let's take a moment to explore this mental space a bit. Envision a dark, stuffy attic crowded with all sorts of things saved from the past: old pictures of events and people, some bringing happy memories, others painful memories; old clothes and shoes that don't fit anymore; rusty, outdated tools; broken-down furniture; knickknacks from who knows where; and old presents just waiting to be regifted. This musty old attic is so cluttered that there's no room to move and no room to store anything new. It's overflowing with elements of the past.

The mind is a lot like this attic: so chaotic and filled with what has happened that it isn't possible to respond to the flow of life with a fresh perspective. Each experience is solidified and carefully preserved, and reactions to new experience are informed by those precious possessions—the accumulation of your feeling and thought stuff. This accumulated stuff represents layer upon layer of disconnection from life, from others, and from yourself. And yet each layer is what you consider to be your life.

Think of how liberating it would be to go into this attic and start to clear out the clutter. That's exactly what this next practice will do. It will allow you to declutter your mind so that you can see the flow of your life clearly and respond to what's currently happening, rather than viewing events through the lens of the past and reacting on the basis of thoughts and feelings that don't have a genuine bearing on the present.

❧ PRACTICE: Watching, Naming, and Letting Go ❧

This practice is similar to the movie theater practice you've done before, with a new twist. This time, you'll practice greeting each thought, emotion, and sensation. You'll watch it, name each with a single word, and then let it go. Some people have told me they find it useful to visualize writing each name on a balloon and then releasing it, or to visualize writing the name on a leaf and letting it float away down a stream. These are just a few ideas. Feel free to come up with your own. Whatever imagery you use, this practice is an effective means of clearing away some of the clutter from the insistent chatter of big deal mind, allowing you to experience more spaciousness.

Assume the attitude of mindfulness, closing your eyes, relaxing your muscles, and resting comfortably for a few minutes.

You can use the movie theater image or any image that works for you. The goal is to simply be present and watch the parade of your thoughts, emotions, and sensations without judgment, reaction, or distraction. Simply watch whatever passes through your awareness and greet each internal event gently with a "hello."

After greeting each internal event, give it a name and then let it go. For example, if a conflict that occurred yesterday passes through, greet it with a "hello," then just name it "conflict" and let it keep passing by. Then another awareness arises, perhaps impatience. Greet it gently, then name it ("impatience") and let it go. Use nouns, not adjectives, as you name your experiences. That way you'll simply be stating what it is without opinion, reaction, or judgment.

It's common for certain internal events to reappear time after time. That's fine. Remember, that too is an opportunity for mindfulness. If something keeps returning, just name it without judgment, reaction, or distraction. If impatience keeps returning, just name it "impatience," not "that damn impatience again." Be open and curious in regard to things that come up repeatedly. Perhaps these are things that need deeper attention.

After watching your thoughts for at least five minutes, take some time to contemplate and answer the following questions.

What did you notice about your thoughts, emotions, and sensations as you named them and let them go?

_____

_____

_____

_____

As you continued with this practice, did you notice a shift? If so what was it like?

_____

_____

_____

_____

Did certain thoughts, emotions, and sensations continually return? If so, what were they? What could they be asking you to pay attention to in your life? Is there anything that you've been ignoring or disconnected from?

_____

_____

_____

_____

If you didn't experience a shift, don't concern yourself with it. Just continue doing this practice; eventually you'll find your way to the shift. Keep in mind that developing mindful responses to your experience is a lifelong process. It isn't like a switch that flips, instantly transporting you to some magical place.

THE VALUE IN ACKNOWLEDGING YOUR EXPERIENCE

The preceding practice will help you cultivate the skill of simply acknowledging your internal experience with a genuine expression of interest that's based in patience, openness, and compassion. The aim isn't to accept or reject. Doing so would create a duality based on preferences, which only serves to maintain solid self and fear-based reactions to experiences deemed unacceptable.

Here's an example: Jeff used to get angry with drivers who pulled out in front of him. He was concerned about his road rage and decided to see if mindfulness might be helpful. He learned to label his thoughts, feelings, and actions: anger, tension in his shoulders, frustration, judgment, name-calling, rapid breathing, and so on. As he practiced observing and labeling these events, he experienced how his reactiveness lost its influence. The other driver became just another driver. In fact, he found that it hardly perturbed him when someone pulled out in front of him. As he came to see his life as a continual flow, episodes of other drivers pulling out in front of him quickly receded into his past, rather than being frozen in space and time and carried along into subsequent experiences.

Instruction in mindfulness often directs people to be in the presence of their experiences without judgment, reaction, or distraction. Yet your experience may very well involve being judgmental, reactive, or distracted. The aim is not to erase these experiences, but to simply note them without becoming attached to them or getting caught up in them. Mindfulness is tricky in this way. Trying to do something (paying attention) while also trying *not* to do something else (being judgmental and reactive) splits your experience between what is acceptable and what isn't. Working on creating spaciousness is the key, as it allows all aspects of your experience to coexist and be grist for the mindfulness mill. Remember, mindfulness isn't about imposing one experience upon another; rather, it's about remaining present to the flow of your experience without resorting to fear-based, mindless reactions.

Saying hello to internal events allows you be aware of your internal world so that you can respond mindfully to every aspect of your experience—even those aspects you have traditionally attempted to reject, deny, or discount. Including all elements of your experience on your path to mindfulness invites you to cultivate great love and compassion, first for yourself and then radiating outward, ultimately to encompass all living beings. There is nothing to be accepted and nothing to be rejected, just every moment to be embraced with spacious, mindful presence and great care.

SUMMARY

When you create spaciousness, you allow what I refer to as "something larger" to articulate in your life. You may call this something larger by any number of names, such as God, the universe, Tao, the void, Buddha mind, heaven, nirvana, or nothingness. The name isn't important. The experience is. We are all deeply connected, and interconnected to all of life. Mindlessness disconnects you from this something larger, and spaciousness is the antidote: a powerful way to reconnect and experience the wonder, compassion, and brilliance you represent in the ongoing process of the evolution of something larger.

CHAPTER 3

Relaxing Your Breath and Body

The breath, the body, and mindfulness are inextricably linked. Learning how to breathe spaciously will create a strong foundation you can build on as you cultivate patient, open, and compassionate responses. Right now, pause for a moment and just check in with your breath. Don't do anything to try to change it, just sit and watch it. Notice the natural flow: in, out, in again, out again. Next, notice how the muscles in your face, neck, and shoulders feel. If your breathing is shallow and rapid, you probably have at least a low level of tension throughout the body. Bringing your breath to a deeper place, as you'll learn to do in this chapter, has a powerful ability to help relax this muscular tension.

If it seems strange that something as simple as breathing can have such profound effects, think for a moment how frequent and continuous the breath is. On average, people take between twelve and fifteen breaths per minute. So if you're thirty-five years old, you will have already taken somewhere around 250 million breaths. Just imagine how powerful it would be if you could use any given breath as a way to connect with a more mindful, spacious life experience.

THE BREATH AND THE BODY AS ANCHORS

You probably usually take your breath for granted. Breathing is just something you do automatically and without much thought—mindlessly, really. Yet its inherent rhythm is a gentle reminder of the flow your life naturally expresses. Consider that you take about nineteen thousand breaths each day. This gives you a multitude of opportunities to connect with your breath as an anchor.

Your breathing is influenced by the way you perceive your environment. If you view your environment (including events in your inner world) as threatening, your SNS is activated, which results in rapid, shallow breathing. On the other hand, when you increase the supply of oxygen to your mind-body system, you elicit a powerful psychophysiological response that serves to calm your SNS, reducing fear-based, reactive mindlessness. In this chapter, I'll teach you a breathing technique I've developed over the years that can enhance your oxygen levels and reduce your reactivity. It also provides an introduction to a concept I call *the pause*. I'll develop this concept in detail as the book unfolds. For now, know that the pause is an important experience to embrace as you continue to develop spaciousness and live more mindfully.

Similarly, checking in with your body, focusing on its sensations, and mindfully releasing tension is also a powerful way of developing mindfulness and enhancing your sense of spaciousness. By checking in to see whether and where you have any tension, pain, or other physical sensations, you can gain a greater understanding of how you tend to react to various life experiences. You can then use this understanding as a signal of your internal state and reactions. Then, using mindful breathing and an intention to release any tension, you can begin to free yourself from these reactions and foster a physiological state in which you're more apt to respond, rather than react, to life events.

THE BREATH OF A CHILD: CENTER POINT BREATHING

Center point breathing began one night twenty-eight years ago when I was a new father watching my firstborn sleep in her crib. Alone in the softly lit room, I was entranced by the simple silence of her sleeping. As time went on, I noticed I had begun breathing along with her, at her rhythm and pace. Two things became evident: The first was how naturally she breathed from her belly (this type of breathing is often called diaphragmatic breathing). At that time in my life, I was very active in yoga and familiar with this sort of breathing, so this was a comfortable place to return to. The second thing I noticed, much to my amazement, was a pause at the end of each of her out breaths. She would inhale, exhale, and then pause and rest gently and quietly, as if waiting for her next in breath to arrive. Then she would inhale, exhale, and pause and rest again, and again, and again.

In that moment, it dawned on me that most of us waste the opportunity to rest with our naturally occurring pauses. Many of the breathing techniques I had learned focused on the pause at the end of the in breath; now I experienced the intensity of the pause that arrives naturally at the end of each out breath.

The center point approach to breathing is a powerful method of experiencing spaciousness, yet it's also very easy to learn. One of the wonderful aspects of this breathing practice is that you can do it anywhere, anytime. You need not close your eyes or adopt an unusual posture, so you can practice breathing in this way while doing the dishes, driving, arguing with your fifteen-year-old son, or any other time you'd like to remain in a spacious, receptive, and open stance in regard to whatever is occurring at the moment, without reaction, judgment, or distraction.

∾ PRACTICE: Center Point Breathing ∾

Too often, people breathe primarily into their shoulders and upper chest, which doesn't allow as much oxygen to enter the lungs. When you breathe with only a third or at best half of your lung capacity, your oxygen levels become depleted, activating the sympathetic nervous system. Think of it this way: If you use only one-third of your lung capacity when you breathe, this means that the 75 trillion cells in your body are being asked to get by on two-thirds less oxygen. The entire body registers this as a state of stress, fear, and distress. Paradoxically, and unfortunately, this keeps your breathing rapid and shallow.

This practice will help you recalibrate your breathing and return to natural belly breathing. As mentioned, this is also called *diaphragmatic breathing*, a reference to the diaphragm muscle, which separates the chest and abdominal cavity. When you breathe fully, the diaphragm expands down into the abdomen to allow the lungs to fully inflate. A word of caution with this practice: If you suffer from any sort of respiratory distress, such as asthma, pneumonia, chronic obstructive pulmonary disease, or bronchitis, push out only as much air as comfortable when you exhale, because pushing all of your air out could create greater distress.

1. *Assume the attitude of mindfulness and take a few minutes to rest there, breathing easily and focusing gently on the rhythm of your breath.*

2. *Focus on the next arriving in breath, then exhale completely, using your stomach muscles to push all of the air out. When you have expelled as much air as possible, hold for a second or two.*

3. *Allow air to return naturally to your lungs. Don't suck air in, as this will most likely create a hyperventilation response. Just allow your lungs to gently fill back up.*

4. *Exhale and inhale naturally for one breath.*

5. *Once again exhale completely, pushing all of the air out and trying to push out a bit more air this time than the previous time. Hold for a second or two, then allow your lungs to fill with air naturally.*

6. *Exhale and inhale naturally for one breath.*

7. *Two more times, go through this cycle of forced exhalation, a brief hold, natural inhalation, and natural exhalation and inhalation. This makes a total of four cycles.*

8. *At the end of the fourth cycle, just breathe comfortably in whatever rhythm feels natural. Be aware of what your breath is like as you breathe naturally, and direct your attention to the pause that occurs at the end of each out breath. Rest comfortably in that pause and wait until your next in breath arrives.*

    Be aware of what your experience is like as you rest with that pause. Bring your attention to how you feel emotionally and physically and to what's happening to your big deal mind. If your attention wanders, gently remind yourself to return to the pause.

9. *After observing your pause over the course of a few minutes, take some time to explore and answer the following questions.*

After completing four cycles of center point breathing, what did you notice about the rhythm of your breath?

_____

_____

_____

_____

_____

What did you notice about any physical sensations you experienced while breathing in this way?

_____

_____

_____

_____

_____

When you began noticing and accentuating the pause at the end of the out breath, what did you experience at first?

_____

_____

_____

_____

_____

As you continued to rest with the pause, what began to occur physically? Did you notice your shift? How?

_____

_____

_____

_____

_____

As you rested with the pause, did the pause change in any way?

_____

_____

_____

_____

_____

For the next week, practice center point breathing two times each day, and then continue to practice center point breathing on a regular basis—as you're working through this book, and afterward. It takes only a few minutes, and the repeated practice will benefit you for the rest of your life, as you'll be able to return to that pause with just the simple inquiry "Where is my pause?" Whenever you practice this breathing technique, direct your attention to both the physical and emotional aspects of the experience. There may be some sort of resistance, especially at first. This is natural, since this is a new and often foreign type of breathing. If it does feel foreign, realize that this is because you've become accustomed to breathing with only a limited portion of your lung capacity. Recalibrating the breath can feel strange at first. I encourage you to be patient; eventually your mind-body system will remember that this type of breathing is what is natural.

This simple technique provides two key benefits: It helps you directly experience the balancing of your autonomic nervous system, and it empowers you to maintain a posture of responsiveness amidst your life experiences, without judgment, reaction, or distraction. You no longer have to suffer passively when fear or anxiety strikes. When you become comfortable with resting in your pause, it can provide a space where you can gain a new perspective on existing concerns.

Anita's Story

Anita, a thirty-one-year-old single woman who works as a nursing assistant at a nursing home, was engaged in a serious struggle with anxiety and panic, experiencing panic attacks a few times every week. During our first session, she repeatedly stated that her family had anxiety problems and therefore this was in her genes. She told of how her mother, aunt, and two sisters struggled with panic and anxiety and said, "Nothing worked for them so I suppose that nothing will work for me. I've been this way for as long as I remember. My mom says that I was very anxious as a child. I've been to other therapists and psychiatrists and they haven't been able to help me, so I doubt you will be able to help, either." Anita seemed very attached to this notion of her anxiety being part of her genetic makeup.

I acknowledged her suffering, and her persistence and efforts in trying to get rid of her symptoms, then asked Anita if she'd be interested in trying something different—something that wasn't about trying to fight with the anxiety. I suggested that a new approach might be helpful, since her anxiety was so strong and had defeated many qualified and capable therapists.

I explained how anxiety leads to rapid, shallow breathing, and how this can exacerbate the anxiety. Then I explained center point breathing and how it could help her with her episodes. She was interested but told me, "I'm at a seven out of ten on my anxiety scale right now, so I don't know how well this will work."

I walked Anita through the process and allowed her to feel the change in the depth of her breath. She had never experienced her breathing as coming from her abdomen and remarked on how natural and comfortable it felt. Then I brought her attention to the pause at the end of her out breath and invited her to find a sense of resting there.

She commented on how this pause got longer and longer and how relaxed she became. She then shared, "My anxiety is about a two or three. Wow! I never thought I could bring my anxiety down this far so fast!"

I encouraged her to practice center point breathing twice a day for a week to become familiar with this space. Then, instead of letting her anxiety and panic run away with her, she could recenter by simply asking herself, "Where's my pause?"

Several sessions later, Anita remarked that she was no longer afraid of her anxiety. Whenever she felt it coming on, she returned to her pause and rested there until the anxiety diminished. "Well, I guess this anxiety thing isn't in my genes after all!"

❧ PRACTICE: Watching the Breath ❧

Here's another, more traditional breathing practice. It's similar to the thought-watching practice in chapter 2, but in this case the breath is the focus of your attention. Your breath is a wonderful teacher, being directly linked to the ongoing flow of the rhythm of your life. Breathe in, breathe out, and remember, with about nineteen thousand breaths each day, you have a multitude of opportunities to connect with your life as a flow, an ongoing process. Just as you would never try to stop the ongoing flow of your breath, realize you cannot halt or even dictate the flow of your life. They are one and the same.

Assume the attitude of mindfulness.

Gently bring your attention to the rhythm of your breath and just watch it, without trying to change it in any way. It may be deep, it may be shallow, it may be fast, or it may be slow. Just watch.

Each time your mind drifts somewhere, gently bring it back to simply watching your breath.

You will do this again and again and again; it's the human condition. What's important is bringing your attention back to the focus—in this case, your breath as you breathe naturally. A helpful technique is to simply name the breaths. On the in breath simply say "breathing in," and on the out breath simply say "breathing out."

Watch your breath for about five minutes, then take some time to explore and answer the following questions.

As you gently attended to your breath, what did you notice about its rhythm?

_____

_____

_____

_____

_____

After your attention drifted, what happened to your thoughts as you gently brought your attention back to your breath?

_____

_____

_____

_____

_____

Identify three areas in your life where you'll use this practice to remind yourself of the flow of your life, so as not to get caught up in passing thoughts.

_____

_____

_____

_____

_____

As you watch your breath in daily life, and particularly in the three areas of your life recorded above, be sure to notice how focusing on your breath and returning to your breath affect you—physically, mentally, emotionally, or in any other regard. Take some time to write about what you experience with this practice.

AWARENESS OF PHYSICAL SENSATIONS

As discussed in chapter 1, the fight, flight, or freeze response has impacts throughout the mind-body system. By tuning in to the physical sensations you feel as a result of difficult situations, you can identify your own personal indicators that you're reacting rather than responding. While certain physiological reactions to stress are typical and nearly universal, such as elevated heart rate, muscular tension, and rapid, shallow breathing, we are all unique. Be on the lookout for these "usual suspects," and also study what's typical for you. Perhaps you tend to clench your jaw, or maybe your stomach feels queasy. Once you've identified how you generally respond, you can use these sensations as a signal reminds you that you may be falling into a fear-based reaction. This valuable information reminds you to connect with your breath and your pause, inviting a shift to activity of the parasympathetic nervous system. This will calm your body and allow you to enter a more mindful space.

∾ PRACTICE: Releasing Physical Tension and Distress ∾

This is a traditional practice for mindfulness of the body in which you mindfully breathe, scan your body, and release any tension. As you focus on each part of your body, you'll inhale healing, then exhale tension, distress, and discomfort. If you like, you can visualize healing as a golden light, positive energy, love and compassion, or anything that works for you. You may need to direct several cycles of breath to any given region before it feels relaxed and suffused with healing energy. Once that happens, move on to the next body part. As you move through your body, bring special focus to any areas causing you particular difficulty and distress, and visualize them receiving relief, healing, and vitality.

1. *Lie down, make yourself comfortable, and then adopt the attitude of mindfulness. Stay with this for a few minutes, resting in your breath and calming your mind.*

2. *Focus upon your breath, feeling it throughout your body.*

3. *Focus on your feet, feeling the sensations in your feet for about twenty seconds. Breathe in comfort and healing, and breathe out tension and distress. Stay with your feet until they feel saturated with calm and relaxation.*

4. *Direct your attention to your calves and concentrate on the sensations you feel there for about twenty seconds. Breathe in comfort and healing, and breathe out tension and distress. Stay with your calves until they are full of relaxation and ease.*

5. *Direct your attention to your thighs and concentrate on the sensations you feel there for about twenty seconds. Breathe in comfort and relaxation, and breathe out tension and distress. Stay with your thighs until they feel completely calm and relaxed.*

6. *Move up to your torso, from your abdomen and lower back all the way up to the top of your shoulders. Concentrate on the sensations you feel throughout your torso for about twenty seconds, then breathe in comfort and healing and breathe out tension and discomfort. Stay with your torso until it feels suffused with calm and relaxation.*

7. *Bring your attention to your arms, extending it all the way out to your hands. Concentrate on the sensations you feel throughout your arms for about twenty seconds, then breathe in healing and breathe out tension and discomfort. Stay with your arms and hands until they feel a deep sensation of calm and relaxation.*

8. *Move your attention up to your neck and head, paying particular attention to your face, especially around your mouth, jaw, and eyes. Concentrate on the sensations you feel throughout your neck and head for about twenty seconds, then breathe in comfort and healing and breathe out tension and distress. It's said that simply smiling can promote health and happiness, so suffuse your face with a sensation of well-being—a glow that's akin to a smile.*

9. *Expand your attention to take in sensations throughout your entire body, including any remaining tension and discomfort. Breathe in healing and ease and breathe out tension and distress. Stay with this until your entire body feels deeply relaxed and suffused with healing energy.*

10. *Remaining connected with your breath, take a moment to be with your body and feel a growing sense of oneness—that everything is connected. Rest and let any sensation come to you, accepting that it is part of you, no matter what it is.*

11. *When you're ready, open your eyes, sit up slowly, then take some time to contemplate and answer the following questions.*

Reflect on and describe the change between how your body felt at the beginning of this practice and how it felt at the end.

_____

_____

_____

_____

What areas experienced the most release or relief? What was that like for you?

_____

_____

_____

_____

Where in your body did you notice particular distress? As you focused on those parts with healing attention, what did you notice about how you felt about that part of your body and its distress?

_____

_____

_____

_____

What did you notice as tension and distress were released and you began to feel reconnected to your body?

_____

_____

_____

_____

When you finished the body scan, what areas still had stress and discomfort? What thoughts, feelings, or experiences do you imagine are being stored in those areas?

_____

_____

_____

_____

One of the benefits of releasing physical tension is that it can also release feelings of solidity that have accumulated in response to fear, stress, and discomfort. As you practice bringing mindful attention to your body, you will be less likely to react to life events with physical symptoms and sensations such as tightness, rapid heart rate, stomach upsets, and headaches. Being more free of this burden, your body will be more sensitive to the flow of all aspects of your life, allowing you to bring mindful responses to whatever you encounter. You'll also feel more at ease in your body and calmer, both physically and mentally.

That said, be patient with yourself. Don't impose any expectations that this practice will eliminate all of your physical pain and difficulties. Like all the other mindfulness practices in this book, healing through mindfulness of the body is an ongoing process. If some areas still feel suffering and distress after you practice this body scan the first time, just acknowledge this and affirm your intention to continue this healing practice. Extend the same patience, openness, and compassion to your body experiences as you would bring to any other experience life offers.

SUMMARY

Remaining connected to your breath and your pause provides a gentle and ever-present reminder of the flow of your life. And because your breath and body are always with you, you can take center point breathing and other practices involving mindfulness of the breath and body with you everywhere you go As you move forward into part 2 of this book, some of the work will be challenging. We'll be looking at big deal mind and its strategies for keeping you caught up in its big deals rather than being mindfully present as your life unfolds. As you do this work, clear seeing will help you cultivate awareness of what's actually occurring and allow you to take a creative and dynamic approach to dealing with big deal mind and its strategies. Big deal mind may feel threatened by the work in part 2 of this book, and you may feel your SNS becoming activated. Whenever this happens, that would be a good time to bring awareness to physical sensations and practice some center point breathing.

Common Obstacles
to Mindfulness

The next four chapters explore four tricky techniques that big deal mind uses to protect solid self: illusions, delusions, attachments, and aggression. I think of each of these as a veil—something that conceals, separates, or screens out. Illusions, delusions, attachments, and aggression all interfere with clear seeing by providing a perspective on your experiences that can be radically different from what's actually occurring, which has the effect of separating you from the ongoing flow of your life. These four veils are interwoven and often interdependent. When illusions are challenged, delusion steps in to explain the discrepancy between the illusions and reality, and then resistance to any information to the contrary shows up as attachment. Ultimately, aggression steps in to protect all three. The journey though illusion, delusion, and attachment generally occurs so quickly that we don't recognize their influence until they show up in aggressive mindless reactions. In this part of the book, I'll help you slow this process down and separate out its elements so you can practice clear seeing with each of them.

When I was a boy, I taught myself to play the drums. At first, I'd just put on an album and try to figure out what the drummer was doing. But even though I could hear the end result, I had no clue about how it was accomplished. Then I realized I could play the album at a slower speed so I could hear each individual strike of the drumsticks. I played along at this slower speed until I got it, and with time and practice I found I could hear what was going on at a normal speed. In the following chapters I offer you a similar experience—in this case slowing down the habitual and rapid progression through illusion, delusion, attachment, and ultimately aggression.

CHAPTER 4

Illusion

Illusion is about misperception and generally involves considering yourself and your experiences to be permanent, lasting, and solid. Big deal mind, which I'll also refer to as illusion mind throughout this chapter, thrives on creating and maintaining this illusion of permanence and solidity. However, perceiving that your experience, and even your identity, is lasting and permanent creates a conflict between your perception and your actual experience, and this can cause you to resist the flow of your life.

When your attitudes and perceptions repeatedly collide with the flow of experiences that actually comprise reality, suffering is the result. In this chapter, you'll learn to let go of your attachment to a sense of solid self, which results in separateness and duality, and instead create a sense of spaciousness even in the presence of your illusions. This spacious perspective will allow you to see beyond your illusions and know them for what they are, clearing the way for you to experience how patient, open, and compassionate responses—mindful responses—can emerge in progressively more areas of your life.

LIFE IS NOT AN ILLUSION

You may be familiar with the philosophical concept that life is an illusion and this illusion must be rejected in order to live mindfully. I don't buy this. Rejecting your life as an illusion sets up an internal conflict based on resistance—resistance to the flow of your present moments. Life itself is *not* illusory. The fashion in which life unfolds at any given moment is just fine. It is the way you perceive the events of your life that creates illusion and, as a result, suffering.

The Limits of Human Perception

Take a moment and look at the wall across from you. Notice all there is to notice: color, windows, artwork, wood trim—everything that your eyes register. Now close your eyes for fifteen seconds.

Open your eyes and look at the wall again. Has anything changed? It's likely that your eyes won't detect any differences; however, on another level that your senses can't perceive, the wall is in a constant state of change and even motion. It's actually a collection of vibrating atoms that, by way of their interactions and your perceptual limitations, gives the wall its solid appearance. Because your eyes didn't register any change in the wall, the thinking and analyzing part of your mind concludes that it's the same wall. Make no mistake: The wall is not illusory, but it is ever-changing. The limitations of human visual perception are what creates the illusion of permanence. In a similar way, you try to make sense of your experiences by perceiving them as lasting, permanent, and solid. This isn't a failing on your part; it's a normal process. We all do this. However, learning not to be fooled by it is essential to creating mindful responses to the actual flow of your life. This is where clear seeing comes into play. Understanding the constant flow of all existence is essential to avoiding being hooked by the appearance of solidity.

Another example is the constant flux and change of your thoughts and feelings. Take a moment and reflect: What thoughts were in your mind thirty seconds ago? Three minutes ago? Two hours ago? Five days ago at this time? At the time they probably seemed important, yet now there's a good chance you can't recall them. Where did they go? Did they even exist? Something was happening that you call your thoughts, and at the time, illusion mind insisted that your experience was solid, lasting, and permanent. However, when you examine this, you see clearly how your thoughts and feelings are actually ever-changing and reflect the ongoing flow of your life.

How the Brain Solidifies Experience

Your sensory organs distinguish visual information, sounds, aromas, flavors, and sensations in much the same way as other creatures' do. Your brain registers a tree much the same as a deer, a bear, or a moose registers a tree. The difference in what happens to that information arises because your cerebral cortex is highly developed, which isn't the case for most animals. This brain structure is responsible for how you think about the information that your senses transmit to your brain. The moose can't call what it sees a tree, but you can. Your cerebral cortex names and categorizes what your senses perceive as seemingly fixed, solid, and permanent distinctions: This is a tree; it's a Japanese maple; it's a Higasayama type of Japanese maple; it will grow six- to twelve-feet tall; it is best suited for planting in zones 6 to 9; and so on. This type of naming and categorizing can be valuable, but it also reinforces the illusion of lasting, permanent, and solid experiences and identities.

As you work on drawing back the veil of illusion, don't go overboard. The functions of thinking and trying to make sense out of your environment are a wonderful gift. This is what allows you to become educated, teach your children, balance your checkbook, build a house, fix a leaky faucet, or perhaps perform open-heart surgery. The key is to focus on the ways you apply this ability that contribute to suffering and mindlessness.

When illusion causes you to lose your connection to the natural movement and flow of your experiences, anything that runs contrary to that illusion is perceived as a threat, activating your sympathetic nervous system and generally resulting in fear-based, mindless reactions. In a vicious cycle, this SNS reaction reinforces your illusion that the threat is solid, lasting, and real, and round and round it goes. The more this process is reinforced, the more your perceptual container shrinks. The water starts tasting saltier and saltier, and you're likely to think your difficulties are because of the salt.

Never the Same River

If you take a drink out of a river, then return the next day and take another drink, have you taken a drink from the same river? Paradoxically, yes *and* no. If you look at the river as a fixed concept, then yes, you did take a drink from the same river. There is a name for the river. It was here yesterday, it's here today, and it will be here tomorrow. The naming of the river and all of its components—water, banks, rocks, ripples, bends—creates the illusion of sameness. The process of naming helps create the veil of illusion, implying that whatever is named is solid and unchanging, fixed in space and time.

On another level, if you look deeper at the actual reality of the river, the answer is no. Time, flow, water volume, and erosion have all changed the river. Its temperature, its speed, and even its chemical composition change by the day, hour, minute, and second. Even the simple act of taking a drink out of the river changes it. Mindful living invites us to awaken to and examine this deeper level of the flow of life. It invites us to embrace the wonders of the natural flow of life and the ongoing evolution of all that is.

Mavis and Terry's Story

When Mavis and Terry were getting ready for work one morning, Terry went to the kitchen to make coffee but found they were out. He had asked Mavis to pick up coffee the previous day, and she had told him she would. When Mavis said she'd forgotten, Terry got upset, and his anger spilled over to the other times he felt Mavis had let him down or disappointed him. Mavis became defensive and tried to tell Terry that she'd buy some coffee after work and that he could use the instant coffee in the cupboard if he was desperate, but this didn't placate Terry (especially because of his attachment to good coffee!). The argument continued until they left for work, and Mavis felt frustrated that Terry couldn't seem to let it go.

Throughout the day, Mavis ruminated over the conflict, revisiting the things Terry had said, which further reinforced her opinions about what he'd said. She prepared herself to continue the conflict that evening, rehearsing her retort time and again, listing all the things she did for Terry that he didn't appreciate, and complaining about how critical and unforgiving he was. The conflict became increasingly solidified every time she revisited it, and Mavis carried this solidified experience with her throughout her day.

After work, Mavis was poised with her well-rehearsed script when Terry walked through the door. But before she could speak, Terry said, "Mavis, I am so sorry I ripped into you this morning. The argument ruined my whole day. I tried to call you, but you were in meetings. I hate it when we leave for work arguing. I know I forget to do things too, and it was unfair for me to react the way I did. And you know what? I can pick up coffee at the store just as easily as you can. I don't know why I made such a big deal of this—it's just coffee!"

Mavis was slack-jawed. This wasn't the Terry she'd carried with her all day. Where did that yelling, criticizing Terry go? She was so ready, but for what? For a solidified interaction and slice of time that no longer existed. Mavis's big deal mind had frozen Terry and the argument in space and time. Her veil of illusion insisted that the Terry of that morning was going to be the Terry of the evening. In her mind, the angry Terry was a solid and permanent entity. When she got home, she was ready to pick up the conflict that had occurred nine and a half hours ago as though no time had passed. What she discovered was that Terry wasn't the same person he had been that morning. He had softened. She hadn't.

The Limitations of Solidified Experience

When a fear reaction kicks in, you're likely to freeze your experiences in space and time, creating the illusion of yourself and your experience as solid and permanent. As a result, you'll continue to interact with yourself, others, or the situation as though they remain in a frozen state. Consider a girl who was bitten by a dog as a child. At age thirty-three, dogs still rekindle her protective fear reaction. Since one dog bit her, she perceives that all dogs will bite her. This experience has been frozen; she carries it with her through space and time, and it interferes with her ability to learn new responses. Solidifying experiences in this way leaves no room for being open to the actual events of your life and ultimately keeps you locked into fear-based reactions disconnected from the situation at hand.

Like a river, each human life is actually a series of moments linked together in seeming continuity. Yet when you look more deeply, you can see that the life of today is different from that of yesterday, or even an hour or a minute ago. Life changes continuously from moment to moment. When you accept the reality of change and impermanence, you experience your life more as a flow and can respond to your experiences with greater flexibility and compassion.

❧ PRACTICE: Observing Impermanence ❧

This practice will help you develop your awareness of the ever-changing quality of your experience. As you become more sensitive and attuned to the impermanence inherent in all things, your vision will be less clouded by the veil of illusion, allowing you to more easily avoid becoming ensnared by big deal mind. I suggest a mall or shopping center for this practice because these environments are often so rich in sensory stimuli. However, any crowded place will do, such as an airport, a coffee shop, or a sidewalk on a busy street. Whatever place you choose, make sure you'll feel comfortable sitting, observing, and writing in your journal.

Take your journal or a notebook and go visit a local mall or shopping center. Find a place to sit, then adopt the attitude of mindfulness and allow your senses to simply register everything that's going on around you. First spend time taking in all that your eyes see. Just let your eyes see without looking at anything. Then apply this approach to your other senses in turn: hear without listening to anything; sense things without feeling for them; and let your nose register aromas without naming them. Just notice, don't form opinions or judgments, and don't engage in reactions. Take one minute to do this, spending about fifteen seconds with each sense.

Open your journal and, without looking up during the process, begin writing about everything you saw, heard, felt, and smelled. You don't have to write complete sentences; words or phrases will do. If you saw a woman in a blue top, just write "woman in blue top," or even just "blue top." If you heard someone laugh, write "laughter." If you smell coffee, just write "coffee." If you did form opinions or judgments (which might be inevitable), don't write them down. Don't write what you thought of the blue top, the laughter, the coffee. Keep writing until you've listed everything that you recall your senses having experienced. Then close your journal.

Take a few moments to just sit as you normally would. Look around, and get up and stretch if you like. Allow about five minutes to pass.

Take a deep breath, return to the same place where you sat before, then look around again and absorb all that your senses register, once again taking about a minute and spending about fifteen seconds with each sense. Then open your journal and once again write down everything you observed—just the facts, without opinions or judgments. Keep writing until you've listed everything you experienced this second time.

Go back and read your first entry, then your second entry, and then take some time to contemplate and answer the following questions.

What similarities did you notice between the first entry and the second?

_____

_____

_____

_____

What differences did you notice between the two entries?

_____

_____

_____

_____

Did each entry reflect the same experience? If not, why?

_____

_____

_____

_____

_____

What was it like to observe without opinions and judgments?

_____

_____

_____

_____

_____

Maintaining sensory openness during this practice allows your experience to be more connected with the actual moment-to-moment flow of your life. In this brief practice, you experienced how much a situation can change. You can use this as a reminder of the ever-changing nature of reality when your illusion mind wants to hold things as solid in space and time. Use it as a touchstone for remembering to look at everything and everyone with clear seeing, perceiving the flow of moments as they unfold in your life.

There's good reason for that familiar maxim "Never go to bed angry." If you go to bed angry, you solidify that experience and carry it into the next day. So if you're angry with your spouse or partner, when you wake up and see that person the next morning, you're likely to react as you did yesterday. Rather than relating mindlessly that way, bring the awareness you cultivated with this practice into your daily life, embracing each moment with a sense of newness that will enliven your life.

How Illusions Cause Problems

Your perceptual abilities limit what you can see of the natural universe. Remember, it took a very long time for us humans to realize that the earth isn't stationary, with everything else revolving around it. Rather, the earth is in constant motion within our solar system, and the solar system is in motion as well, and so on.

One of the major problems with illusion mind is the false sense of security it creates. You come to rely on this illusory security and define yourself and your life from this perspective: "I have a college education. I'm a successful contractor. My son is starting quarterback on his football team. I drive a Hummer. We're going to Hawaii next month." But what happens when events arise and you can't afford the gas for your Hummer and you have to cancel your trip? Think back on your own life and notice how you've reacted to having to let go of something you had counted on—something illusion mind had made solid. When you relate to your world and the people in it as a collection of things to have or possess, they lose their "being sense" and take on a lifeless quality devoid of any relational importance. This illusion of solidity gives a false sense of safety, definition, and security.

For example, the illusion that youthfulness must be preserved at all costs lies behind a plethora of diets, cosmetics, surgeries, and supplements that offer the promise of standing outside of time, fixed and unchanging. Obviously, you know that you'll grow old and eventually die. However, the fear of this inevitability serves to solidify your experiences and compel you to attempt to resist the flow of time. The next time you go to the grocery store, take a moment and examine the covers of the magazines and tabloids that line the checkout row. First of all, you might note that the pictures are frozen images. Then notice what the words are saying about the images you see. If you aren't mindfully aware, you may end up freezing this image in your awareness and carrying it around with you as a criterion against which you measure yourself. This solidifying is the foundation of your suffering.

Illusion and the Solid Self

The veil of illusion also conceals and distorts your sense of self. To understand how, let's first look at the term "self." Self comprises the collection of thoughts, feelings, memories, and experiences that have been solidified into a defined sense of who you are. This sense of self is experienced as a fixed entity. Because of the illusion of permanence, solid self doesn't flow with experiences; rather, it collides with them like a bumper car, bouncing from one experience to the next, aiming at one and trying to avoid another. Not only are you bumping into your own experiences, other people's experiences are also bumping into you. When solid self attempts to protect itself from any threat that would challenge its solidity, it creates a sense of disconnect, a duality of me versus you, or me versus my experience. With each bump, not only does your self feel increasingly more solid, other people and your experiences feel more solid too.

Illusion mind keeps you separate from the experiences in your life. When everything is solid and every experience and interaction feels like a jolt, your sympathetic nervous system remains activated. This reinforces the veil of the illusion, keeping you stuck in fear-based, mindless reactivity. Everything you perceive as "not you," as separate and distinct, represents a potential threat or danger. Everything that is "not you" can attack you (physically or emotionally), criticize you, expose you, ignore you, abandon you, or defeat you. From this perspective, you lose your sense of connectedness to those around you, to the wider world, and even to yourself.

When you maintain separateness in your life, you operate out of fear, trying to fix things in an attempt to get rid of some problem, pain, situation, or person. With mindfulness, you can simply allow a sense of presence to develop with regard to a particular concern. Rather than rejecting it, pushing it out of your awareness, and disregarding it as part of your experience, you can create a spaciousness that will allow you to soften and be more open and patient.

CLEAR SEEING: LOOKING BEYOND SOLIDITY

From our discussion in chapter 2, recall that clear seeing is simply watching what's occurring, not just in your external environment but also in your thoughts, feelings, and elsewhere in your internal world.

Another aspect of clear seeing is keeping your experience of the world light: operating from a stance of "Gee, I wonder what's happening now. Where is big deal mind going, and what is it trying to get me to focus on?" This simple clear-seeing process keeps you from solidifying your experiences. With clear seeing, you'll be able to notice when and how big deal mind surfaces and how you can resist its seduction. With time, clear seeing may even prevent activation of reactive mind—or at least keep its activity to a minimum.

Clear seeing allows reactive mind to quiet down, thus allowing you to become increasingly attentive to your experience on all levels. This goes a long way toward creating the spaciousness necessary to engage in heartfelt and careful gestures, even in the smallest of actions. A mind that's innocent of preconceptions, judgments, and prejudices allows you to explore and observe things as they are.

The beauty of clear seeing is that it keeps you connected to the ongoing flow of whatever is actually occurring, noticing the way illusion mind solidifies your experiences. Clear seeing allows you to appreciate the dynamic richness of your true self and the world in which you live without getting caught up in the veil of illusion mind.

Francis's Story

Francis, a thirty-one-year-old man, is married with three children. His wife is an accountant, and until recently, Francis worked as a contractor for a successful company and enjoyed a very prosperous life. But due to a downturn in the economy and the building industry, Francis lost his job and soon descended into serious depression. As he discussed his experiences, he frequently used words that reflected the solidity he felt in his life and his body. "I just can't seem to get moving. Some days I don't even have the energy to get out of bed." He also talked about how his life "had ended," saying, "This is the worst thing that could ever happen to me and my family. I am such a failure as a man. Now my wife has to earn all the money so we can pay our bills. The outlook for me is so bleak, and I don't see anything changing. I can't stand going out in public because I don't want people looking at me."

Francis started thinking that if he could just change the "things" in his life, he would be happier. He contemplated selling his truck, his tools, and even his house, and was seriously considering a divorce. When things feel solid, we tend to think that removing them and replacing them with other solid things will lead to happiness. This sort of thinking can extend to people and relationships, even with loved ones. However, things are seldom the problem and certainly weren't for Francis; rather, the source of his distress was his expectation that things and his relationship to them should remain fixed and unchanging, and his belief that undesired changes to his situation made him a failure.

I guided Francis through the theater practice and center point breathing, and he began to practice them regularly. With time, he began to see his life as a flow, rather than an effort to maintain a solid and permanent identity, life, and lifestyle. This allowed Francis to imagine a future with new possibilities. His energy gradually increased, and he began talking with his wife more. Doors opened, opportunities presented themselves, and new directions became clear. He started teaching at a local technical school and also found a part-time job in maintenance at a local high school. These two "temporary experiences," as he called them, showed him that he was interested in a career in teaching. He really enjoyed his contact with young people and helping them by sharing his knowledge in his field of expertise.

During one of our last sessions, he reflected on how things had been changing even when he was convincing himself that they weren't: "Although I felt stuck and solid, life was in the process of moving me along. The more I could stay with my pause, the more I clearly saw how there were choices and options. Who would have thought I would want to be a teacher? Now, no matter what's going on in my life, I can just be patient and wait, because something else is about to occur. I'm much more curious and positive, and my wife notices it too. And sometimes when she gets down or worried, I remind her, "Just wait a few moments, and this will change too."

❧ PRACTICE: Clear Seeing with Illusions ❧

During this practice, you'll bring a difficult situation to mind, then use clear seeing to help you gain spacious presence in regard to the situation, which illusion mind has probably solidified and presented as a threat. As you've built your mindfulness practice, you may have found that certain approaches help you connect with your capacity for clear seeing; use whichever one you find most helpful. If in doubt, use the theater practice introduced in chapters 1 and 2 to step back from your illusions and simply observe them.

In all of the practices in this part of the book that involve bringing difficult situations to mind, please don't judge yourself or shrink away from being present with this situation. Responding mindfully requires that you find the space to be present even amidst difficult internal experiences, including your illusion mind processes.

As with all practices that focus on difficult or painful issues, and particularly all of the practices in part 2 of the book, be gentle with yourself. Start with a situation that's only moderately difficult. Later, you can build on your success and try this approach with more challenging situations, keeping in mind that situations involving trauma are best approached with the support of a therapist, rather than on your own. Whatever situation you choose, if you find yourself becoming tense or reactive, that would be a good time to practice some center point breathing and reconnect with your pause.

Adopt the attitude of mindfulness. Take a couple of slow, easy, deep breaths and let the muscles in your neck, shoulders, and back relax. Reconnect with the rhythm of your breath and your pause, and remain with this rhythm for a couple of minutes.

Now let yourself explore one area in your life that's causing difficulty or frustration—an area where big deal mind has kept your energy focused. It might be a relationship, your health, the economy, a divorce, or the death of a loved one. Spend a couple of minutes with this awareness, connecting with as much sensory information as possible. As you remember this situation, become aware of how you feel it has qualities of solidness and permanence.

You might visualize carefully and patiently holding this concern in your hand. After bringing this situation to mind in detail, apply clear seeing to it using the theater practice or whatever technique works best for you. Stay with this situation for several minutes, then take some time to contemplate and answer the following questions, remaining in this mindful space as you do so.

What do you notice about the way big deal mind contributes to this experience of feeling solid, permanent, and serious? Pay particular attention to how you may feel that the situation is somehow separate from you and therefore experienced as a threat to your happiness.

_____

_____

_____

_____

Use clear seeing to look beyond this situation and explore how your feelings of solidness resist the actual flow of your life. Just describe what you see without judging.

_____

_____

_____

_____

As you stay with clear seeing, notice what begins to come into your awareness that wasn't there before—perhaps a softness, an awareness, or a mindful response.

_____

_____

_____

_____

Consider what your struggle is inviting you to look at. Is there something in your life that you've been ignoring? Remain curious here: "I wonder what I can learn as I apply clear seeing to this situation."

_____

_____

_____

_____

_____

Take this awareness with you in your daily life. From time to time, pause and return to clear seeing so you can explore how the illusion of solidness and permanence is influencing the quality of your life. Stay open and curious with this and embrace the wonder and richness in the ongoing flow of your life. If you notice that you've fallen under the influence of illusion mind and are resisting the flow of your life, don't criticize or judge yourself. Just step back, take a breath, smile, and say to yourself, "Oh, there's illusion mind at work again making things solid and difficult," then return to the flow of your life.

SUMMARY

Illusion is about the perception that people, events, and even your identity are separate, fixed, and unchanging, creating a misleading sense of predictability, sameness, and security. Any threats to these illusions may stimulate the SNS, limiting your ability to respond and potentially reinforcing your fears. As you use clear seeing to contact the reality beyond your illusions, you'll discover new possibilities and doorways. But even though clear seeing can do a great deal to dispel illusion, often the problem is more complex, since illusion is maintained by delusion, typically in the form of the stories we tell ourselves to make sense out of the discrepancy between what we perceive and how the world actually functions. These attempts at making sense often involve solidifying and supporting illusion with beliefs, opinions, judgments, and concepts. The next chapter will help you apply clear seeing to illuminate the reality that lies beyond delusion, but this work may be more challenging, as big deal mind has a greater investment in delusion than illusion and is likely to offer greater resistance to your efforts to cast aside this veil.

CHAPTER 5

Delusion

In this chapter, we'll investigate the ways we use delusions to protect and support illusion mind. Think of delusions as the way you try to explain the discrepancy when your perception of a lasting, permanent, and solid reality is challenged by the way events actually unfold. The word "delusion" often has negative associations, but in the context of this book, I use it simply to describe the stories you tell yourself to explain the vicissitudes of your life. I don't mean to imply that you're delusional as in having a mental illness; it's just that you may be inclined to fool yourself with your stories, as many of us are. There's a big difference.

Delusion and illusion are often presented as the same, but I'm going to make an important distinction between them. Illusion is about misperception. It's an erroneous mental representation. Illusions distort reality, resulting in a mismatch between what is actually occuring and what is perceived. Illusion interferes with mindful responses by solidifying your experiences as lasting and permanent, so that you react to mental constructs, rather than the current reality.

Delusion, on the other hand, is the stories your big deal mind constructs about why your illusions don't match reality. Illusions are often held in the face of evidence to the contrary, and in fact, the more your illusions are challenged, the stronger your stories become. So the veil of delusion is really just stories to reinforce your illusion. They may be statements you say to yourself about someone or something you hold to be true, or basically any beliefs or opinions you've solidified as truth in your mind.

STORIES THAT COMFORT

It may be that some of the stories you've grown accustomed to telling yourself are misleading, and instead of helping you better understand the true nature of reality, they could be contributing to your suffering. Delusion mind can keep you thinking that you're a solid self, a solid thing, and the events and people in your life are likewise felt to be solid, lasting, and permanent. Bear in mind that when you make your thoughts, feelings, and experiences solid, you lay the foundation for suffering.

For example, a man who years ago suffered a very painful divorce may hold onto a story about the court system, attorneys, and perhaps about how he feels about women. As his delusion mind recalls his past, he is likely to project these thoughts and feelings onto the future as stories about why he should never trust relationships, women, attorneys, and so forth. The overall result is his prolonged suffering, as he remains disconnected from his previous life.

Remember, some pain is inevitable. But if you're suffering, it's because your delusion mind has disconnected you from yourself and the flow of your life. Just to be clear, pain and suffering aren't synonymous. Pain is real. It's a physical or emotional message that something is amiss or out of balance. Suffering arises when you struggle with and fight against pain, which increases the focus on the pain and ultimately allows the pain to take on a life of its own. When delusion mind is active, you add layers of opinion, judgment, and reaction to your experience, serving to intensify the suffering associated with pain. You can reduce your suffering by practicing mindful presence—remaining awake, aware, and connected to your life and responding to what is, rather than reacting to the stories which reinforce your fear reaction.

An ancient Zen poem exhorts, "Do not seek the truth, only cease to cherish your opinions." Most of us develop an elaborate scheme of stories on which we rely. When our illusions of the lasting, solid, permanent quality of life are challenged, it can feel easier to close down, resist, and offer an explanation that keeps our sense of control intact rather than respond with patience and openness. Unfortunately, these stories keep us disconnected and closed off from our true life experience.

DELUSIONS AND TIME TRAVEL

Delusion mind is often based on time travel. Many of the stories that remove you from your connection to the dynamic flow of your life are narratives that take you back into your past, or seduce you into a future that hasn't yet occurred—and may not ever occur. Remember, big deal mind's mantra is "Here, pay attention to this," and "this" includes experiences that have already occurred or have yet to occur that you tell yourself stories about. This kind of time travel is one of delusion mind's many tricks to disrupt your connection to the flow of your life.

Time Travel to the Past

When constructing stories to explain why life doesn't match your illusions, you may retreat into your past to retrieve experiences frozen in space and time to use as a comparison to what's happening in the here and now. A common way of doing this is by returning to the "good old days." You may view the good old days through rose-tinted glasses and believe that back then things made sense. That can feel solid, comforting, and better than whatever your reactive mind is resisting in the here and now.

How often do you find yourself having a conversation in your head on your way home from work, perhaps regarding a conflict you had with your supervisor or a colleague? You may not have liked the person's attitude, behavior, or way of handling a situation, and you keep running the situation repeatedly in your mind. This private conversation is the story you tell yourself to help explain why others acted as they did. This reinforces the other as a solid entity. As you know by now, this solidness is often experienced as a threat, stimulating your SNS and limiting your capacity to allow mindful response to emerge. You can become so absorbed in the stories big deal mind is spinning out that you're surprised when you find yourself in your driveway and think, "Wow! I don't remember any of the drive home."

In regard to the past, there's a tendency to think, "Because it was so, it shall always be." Here's an example. When I was in high school, one day I walked past the room where the public speaking class was being taught. The teacher called out my name, asked me to come into the class, and gave me a topic to talk to the class on. (I still remember what it was: How to catch a frog.) He said that I couldn't leave the room until I completed this task. Mortified, I proceeded to mumble, stumble, and dissociate my way through the experience.

Subsequently, every time I had to talk in front of people, I traveled back to this experience and revisited my story that speaking in front of people was worse that death. (This was before I knew that people's fear of public speaking actually is greater than their fear of dying!) I became very clever at coming up with ways I could avoid putting myself in that situation. In college, I didn't take classes that involved talking in front of the class. I turned down being the best man at weddings so I wouldn't have to get up and give a toast. My delusion mind kept telling that same story, which disconnected me from my life as it was for years to come. I built up layers of stories about public speaking that I took to be true, even though all of it was based on just one single event that happened years ago. Mindfulness has been an incredible gift for me in many regards. One is helping my stories lose their powers of time travel. As a result, I've since been able to make presentations and teach at hundreds of seminars, workshops, and retreats, and now I actually enjoy speaking to groups of people!

Beware of becoming invested in narratives you tell yourself about past events over which you had no control, rather than mindfully paying attention to your present experience. This creates layers of disconnection, because the stories you buy into aren't an authentic reflection of your true self or the current situation in which you find yourself. Don't settle for the impacts these stories have on your life. With clear seeing, you can begin to look at how much you've accepted these explanations with little or no examination of whether they hold any truth for you, your authentic self, and your current experience.

Time Travel to the Future

Take a moment to reflect on a time when you were preoccupied about an event in the future, maybe a job interview, a difficult topic you needed to bring up with your spouse or partner, or sending your youngest child off to college. You probably spent a lot of time and energy talking about and rehearsing the event, thinking of what you were going to say, or predicting how things would go. When you construct narratives about the future, delusion mind is attempting to make an event that hasn't even occurred feel as though it's actually going on, potentially leading you to think, erroneously, that it's something you could control.

How many times, after such events have occurred, have you reflected back on whether things unfolded as you anticipated? And think about this: While you're busy anticipating the future, what are you doing as your life is actually unfolding? Remember how Mavis spent the day time traveling to the future and practicing all the ways she was going to respond to Terry about the coffee fiasco? In fact, she was late for a meeting that day because she was sitting in her office, lost in the future, until one of her colleagues came to get her. Her time travel disconnected her not just from the actual passage of time, but also from her life and her responsibilities.

∾ PRACTICE: Identifying Your Stories ∾

This practice will help you apply clear seeing to how delusion mind operates and the ways you use stories to explain your illusions and lend solidity to them. Once again, the theater practice from chapters 1 and 2 is a good way to step back from your stories and simply observe them. If you find yourself becoming tense or reactive during this practice, that would be a good time to do some center point breathing.

> *Adopt the attitude of mindfulness. Take a couple of slow, easy, deep breaths, and let the muscles in your neck, shoulders, and back relax. Reconnect with the rhythm of your breath and your pause, and remain with this rhythm for a couple of minutes.*
>
> *Now begin to explore an area in your life that's a source of difficulty or frustration—an area where big deal mind has kept your energy focused. You might visualize holding this concern in the palm of your hand with great care and patience. Now, staying with your breath, just watch how stories begin to develop around this area of your life. What do you begin to tell yourself about this concern? We all create our own stories, so don't judge or criticize, just keep a curious interest here. Remain in this mindful space for about five minutes, then take some time to consider and respond to the following questions.*

As you hold your concern, what stories do you tell yourself about this concern? Be honest. Your stories may not be pretty; they may reflect a rather dark side. Delusion mind can be very creative at keeping you wrapped up in a self-contained world of reasons, justifications, defenses, and excuses.

_____

_____

_____

_____

_____

How do your stories keep you from experiencing your life as it is, without judgment, reaction, or distraction? How do they make the concern increasingly solid and keep you in a state of fear?

_____

_____

_____

_____

_____

Explore what sort of time travel you employ to remove yourself from your experiences. How do your stories take you to the past? How do your stories take you to the future?

_____

_____

_____

_____

_____

Now let yourself look at where your delusions diverge from what's true and accurate. Examine the differences between what you are telling yourself and what is true about you and your life as it is.

_____

_____

_____

_____

_____

Delusion mind serves to reinforce illusions—the sense of a separate, permanent, lasting, solid experience of life, others, and even oneself. It offers endless stories that function as a type of pacifier. When you learn to recognize these stories for what they are—simply stories you tell yourself—you'll be able to loosen their grip. Again, don't take this as an opportunity to judge yourself. After all, the likely outcome there is feeling threatened and possibly reacting. Rather, maintain a lighthearted fascination where you can say, "Look—there's another story my clever mind has offered. I wonder what's really going on here?"

YOUR BODY SPEAKS

Stories don't reside solely in thoughts and emotions. Big deal mind encompasses the entire psychophysiology, so be careful not to focus solely on the workings of the mind. Our stories can and often do emerge via actual physical expressions.

Your body absorbs the effects of your experiences. You may tend to limit your mindful awareness to how you think and how you feel, emotionally. Language reflects this perspective. We often ask questions such as "What do you think about that?" or "How do you feel about that?" We seldom inquire into what the body went through. And indeed, it would be a bit odd to ask someone, "What did your body think of that?" or "What does your body have to say about that?" Yet your body registers every experience you go through and stores the impacts of your life experiences, albeit in a different way than your mind does. From severe trauma to the day-to-day stresses you encounter, your body stores the remnants of the experiences you go through, yet it seldom gets a chance to express this.

When the body isn't allowed to express the impact of what it has experienced, symptoms may emerge. You can try to silence them with medicines, denial, or self-medication with drugs and alcohol, but these are often yet another veil—one intended to disguise what the body is trying to communicate. The overall effect is that you ignore the importance of the messages your body is sending in an effort to create balance and well-being.

Expanding mindful responses to include your body means approaching the way your body communicates with patience, openness, and compassion. It entails focusing clear seeing on the ways your body expresses the experiences that affect your physiology. When your body isn't feeling or functioning well, you might tend to solidify the experience as something separate—a thing that's happing to you. It isn't unusual to react to these symptoms from a place of fear. As a result, they can become a significant focus of big deal mind.

Don't let delusion mind fool you into thinking that you are different from your body, with the result that you treat your body as a foreign entity. Mindful responding encompasses applying care and loving compassion to how your body goes through this life. Reflect on the practice you learned in chapter 2, in which you watch and name your thoughts and emotions, and how those that persist simply reflect areas that need further attention in your life. The same approach can be applied to physical sensations, as well. In most cases, physical symptoms will persist until you stop and listen to what your body is trying to communicate to you.

Many physical symptoms are treated as though they're due to a mechanical problem. The assumption is if you fix that mechanical problem, your symptoms will go away. However, as our understanding of the mind-body system grows, science is discovering that many symptoms don't fully resolve when only the mechanical aspects of the problem are addressed, and that there is a powerful emotional component to many physical disorders. In fact, entire branches of science, such as psychoneuroimmunology and psychobiology, are dedicated to exploring these connections. It's useful to see symptoms as the actions of a friend, not an enemy. Certain symptoms are, in fact, a natural process of the body attempting to reestablish its balance (Page 1992) and serve a communicative function.

Though physical problems often have physical causes, sometimes there may be an emotional component, and this is always worthy of consideration. For example, a woman came to see me to help her cope with chronic neck pain. She had been to various physicians, chiropractors, and acupuncturists, with little relief. When she focused spacious awareness on being curious about what the pain was trying to get her to pay attention to, she began to clearly see what the pain in her neck was. Her husband had arranged for his disabled brother to come live with them without discussing it with her. She had never been able to give a voice to this story in her life, so it expressed itself as a pain in her neck. It wasn't a mechanical problem; it was the impact of having more responsibilities and worries placed on her without her having a say in the decision. Becoming curious allowed her to better respond to her body with greater care, comfort, and compassion.

A wide variety of symptoms can be related to getting stuck in a certain story. Disorders such as colitis, irritable bowel syndrome, panic attacks, respiratory disorders, sleep problems, startle reactions, fibromyalgia, and chronic fatigue syndrome can all be the body's attempt to tell its story regarding a specific experience. Be sure to bring your mindful awareness and clear seeing to the stories you tell yourself and others about your body. This includes stories about a specific medical condition, such as migraines, arthritis, asthma, or chronic back pain, and also stories about emotional struggles that have a physiological aspect, such as anxiety, depression, sexual abuse, being the child of an alcoholic parent, or concerns about the size, shape, or appearance of your body. Solidified fear experiences often underlie these struggles.

When delusion mind draws you away from the flow of your life and into an experience largely based on fear, it affects the way your body functions. It's worthwhile to periodically ask yourself, "If my body could speak, what would it be trying to get me to pay attention to that I may be ignoring?" This self-inquiry will help you become better acquainted with what symptoms have to tell you about your life and where it might be out of balance.

❧ PRACTICE: Listening When Your Body Speaks ❧

If you have a persistent physical condition, it may be the way your body is trying to deal with a particular story in your life. Clear seeing will help you hear and understand the messages your body is sending, and also help you see how your body may be participating in creating and maintaining your stories.

Assume the attitude of mindfulness and take a couple of slow, easy, deep breaths, then gently bring your awareness to a physical condition you're dealing with. Remaining in this mindful space, take some time to consider and respond to the following questions.

Ask your condition, "If you had a voice and could tell me what you're trying to get me to pay attention to in my life, what would it be?"

_____

_____

_____

_____

_____

As you listened to the story that's embedded in your physical condition, what began to happen to the symptoms associated with that condition?

_____

_____

_____

_____

_____

What did you learn about your physical condition as it relates to a specific story in your life? Does your physical condition contribute to solidifying this story line? For example, does your story line keep you feeling like a victim?

_____

_____

_____

_____

_____

Mindful living involves being spaciously present amidst every aspect of your experiences. This includes embracing the way your body expresses its struggles. It will be helpful to bring clear seeing to the story your body is trying to tell, just as you've learned to observe your thoughts and emotions and respond to them with patience, openness, and compassion.

BRINGING PATIENCE, OPENNESS, AND COMPASSION TO THE BODY

Although patience, openness, and compassion are familiar concepts, in the introduction I took some time to explain their meanings in the context of this book. Since many of us have a hard time accepting our bodies, much less extending patience, openness, and compassion to them, lets revisit these terms and how they apply to the body.

Patience: Spaciousness invites you to be patient with the way your body is at any given time. Rather than treating it as a solid, permanent thing that you have ultimate control over, realize that your body reflects the flow of your life. Be patient with its process. For example, if you wish you weighed less but diets don't seem to work, back off on trying to force the issue using the same strategies. Instead, take care of your body by feeding it healthy foods, taking walks outside on a regular basis, and giving it the rest it needs. And remember, we're all different. Focus on taking care of the body given to you—the one you inhabit now—not on trying to meet come cultural ideal, which is likely to be unrealistic for most of us, anyway.

Openness: Apply the same curiosity to the experiences of your body as you've learned to apply to your thoughts, feelings, and other internal processes, including the activity of big deal mind. For example, be curious about what your body may need from you so it can maintain health and well-being. Rather than fighting your body, figure out how you can support it. Also be curious about the way your body has registered the many experiences in your life. If you have a particular physical condition or difficulty, you can direct your attention to it, bringing spacious curiosity to what your body is trying to express. (The practice just given will guide you in doing this.)

Compassion: As you bring patience and openness to the way your body has absorbed the experiences in your life, you can reintegrate all aspects of your being with your body, allowing it to play a larger and more important role in creating mindful responses. Compassion means treating your body with care and tenderness. It has had to carry you through many challenges and probably hasn't been given the opportunity to tell its story. If you struggle with physical ailments, back off from attempting to silence your body. Instead, embrace it with tenderness and compassion so it can finally feel heard. This is an important step in helping it return to balance and well-being.

SUMMARY

Creating spaciousness will allow you bring clear seeing to your stories and how they serve to maintain your illusions, and therefore your suffering. It will also allow you to see when you're time traveling—living in worries about the future or ruminations about the past, or simply playing out old scripts because those stories are so familiar. As you begin to see the workings of delusion mind, remember to bring compassion to yourself, not judgment and criticism. And don't forget to bring that same attention and compassion to the story your body is attempting to tell. Of course, big deal mind has a lot invested in the delusions it has created. It's natural to want to preserve these stories, as they seem to help maintain a sense of safety and predictability. Yet attachment to these stories only disconnects us from our true selves, our experiences, and our relationships. Fortunately, clear seeing will also allow you to become more aware of your attachments so you can free yourself from the suffering they create.

CHAPTER 6

Attachment

Think of attachment as the energy you put into keeping the veils of illusion and delusion intact. When you attach yourself to the illusion that things, people, or events need to or even *can* remain fixed and unchanging, you lose the ability to see what's actually occurring and respond flexibly and mindfully. Likewise, you can become attached to your delusions—the stories you tell yourself to justify your illusions, even in the face of experience and information to the contrary. As a result, you may end up identifying with a solid self, and seeing your experiences and others as solid, too. This creates a world filled with separateness, duality, and fear, and characterized by suffering.

WHAT IS ATTACHMENT?

While attachment supports both illusion and delusion, there is an exceptionally strong interrelationship between attachment and delusion. As we spend months, years, and even decades buying into certain stories about our identities, others' identities, and the very nature of reality, we become heavily invested in those stories. They become part of our belief system and worldview, and no matter how erroneous they may be, there's an understandable desire to maintain them at all costs. It redeems the time we've invested in them and seems to offer the comforting prospect of living in a world that's predictable. Seeing these stories and beliefs as solid and permanent makes them very important—indeed, essential.

The seed of this sort of attachment is the fear that, in and of yourself, you aren't enough—that deep within you lies some sort of shortcoming or insufficiency, and that "things," whether external and material or internal and conceptual, will make you whole, complete, and "good enough." Let's return to the example of public speaking and the underlying fear "I'm not good enough and everyone in the room will see it." When I give talks on being more confident in public speaking, people often ask, "How can I stand up in front of all those people, knowing how they're thinking about me and judging me?" This reflects a state of fear in which unfounded assumptions about what others are thinking hold more sway over how you feel about yourself than you do. Within this mind-set, others pose a threat to your self-concept.

Attachment can also be seen as a type of grasping: grasping for things, events, beliefs, relationships, or feelings. In order to be attached to these things, you have to experience them as solid. You can be attached to people, possessions, religious or other beliefs, money, and endless other things. Whatever it may be, let's be clear about one point: Even in the case of material objects, you aren't attached to things per se; rather, you're attached to your *ideas* about things and what they represent in the stories you've grown accustomed to telling yourself. This under-scores the important connection between delusion and attachment. Here are some examples:

- You can be attached to your feelings that your partner must never leave you.

- You can be attached to the beliefs of your political party.

- You can be attached to your worry about your new car getting a scratch.

- You can be attached to remaining youthful.

- You can be attached to being right and to your anxiety about being wrong.

- You can be attached to the significance of money, whether it's the money you have or the money you don't have.

Let's explore a common experience of solidifying and becoming attached to images. Advertising is predicated upon freezing images and convincing you to become attached to them. Once you've done so, your big deal mind may maintain a tight grip on them: the status of a shiny new car, the desire for a fabulously attractive body for yourself or your partner, the lure of a large flat-screen television, or even the promise of a wonderful, carefree life if only you'll take a certain medication. These are all frozen images designed to play on our desires and feared inadequacies. But remember, once you purchase that shiny new car and drive it home, it's no longer shiny and new, especially if you live in a snowy area and drive it home in January. You'll arrive home to find it covered in salt, sand, and caked-on muddy snow. Reality confronts your fixed, solid image, and after a year or two, when the dents, dings, and scratches start to accumulate, you're likely to find yourself considering a shiny new car again. As you see, this can be a self-perpetuating cycle.

Plus, this sort of attachment keeps you focused on what you don't have and what you're afraid of losing , so you're likely to overlook what you do have, including the opportunities for feeling whole and fulfilled that are always around and within you.

∽ PRACTICE: Learning What You Cannot Hold ∽

Here's a practice that will help you explore attachment. You'll need to do this in the daytime, and preferably outside in a place where you'll feel comfortable and not self-conscious, such as a deserted field, a grove of trees, or your backyard. Although an outdoor setting is best, you can also do this in a private room in your home.

Bring your attention to the sunlight. Hold your hand out, open and palm up, and let the sun shine on the palm of your hand. Now, try to grab the sunlight. You heard me right: Close your hand and grab the sunlight that's shining on the palm of your hand.

If you're outdoors, open your arms (or just your hands, if this feels less conspicuous) and try to hold on to the breeze. As the breeze blows by, try to hold on to it. (If you're doing this indoors, you can stand near an open window.)

If there are plants nearby—trees, shrubs, flowers, or grasses—bring your awareness to them. Reach out your hand and gently hold on to a petal, a branch, a leaf, a blade of grass. Hold on to it and try to keep it from growing. (Yes, you can injure the plant so it won't grow, but this is an exercise on grasping and attachment, not aggression. That comes in the next chapter.)

Now take some time to contemplate and answer the following questions.

What did you notice as you did this practice? Be honest about all of your reactions. Did you feel calm, agitated, or silly? Did you find yourself reacting with opinions, judgments, or resistance?

Bring your experience of this practice to the ways you grasp and try to hold on to things in your daily life, whether objects, people, situations, thoughts, feelings, or memories. What can this practice teach you about yourself and your way of being in the world?

_____

_____

_____

_____

_____

This experience gets a variety of reactions. What's important here isn't having a particular response to the practice; the aim is to help you become more comfortable with the flow of experiences of your life. It is a bit silly to think that you can hold light (even nuclear physicists can't do that!), the breeze, or the growing of a plant. However, this experience can help you bring clear seeing to how futile it is to try to hold on to or solidify any other aspect of the flow. You can't find security in attempts to hold on to certain thoughts and feelings, you can't hold back the growth and aging of your body to keep it from changing, and you can't hold on to your opinions and beliefs in the hopes that they'll prevent you from being disturbed by the inevitable and eternal process of change. What you can do is develop and expand the spaciousness of your experiential container so that you can respond to whatever arises with greater patience, openness, and compassion. When you aren't blinded by the veil of attachment, your responses will be better matched to what each experience requires.

The Role of Ritual

Your attachments may be revealed by rituals you engage in—everything from formalized holiday or religious rituals to more subtle or trivial rituals, such as always taking the same route to work or beginning your day with a certain routine. A classic example is the rituals athletes engage in as they prepare for a game. Many athletes firmly believe that their rituals influence their performance and the eventual outcome of the game. Consider baseball player Wade Boggs, who ended up with the nickname "Chicken Man" because he ate poultry before every game.

There were other obsessive-compulsive aspects to his routine, such as always taking exactly 150 ground balls during infield practice. He also had a fixation on time. He entered the batting cage at exactly 5:17 p.m. and ran wind sprints at 7:17 p.m. Before each at-bat, he would write the Hebrew word *chai*, meaning "living," into the dirt of the batter's box. When he was playing defense, before each pitch he swiped the dirt in front of him with his left foot, tapped his glove two or three times, and adjusted his cap.

Such attachments are rooted in a fear of not being in control of the outcome of life events. The attached mind prefers superstition and the illusion of security, especially when faced with threatening situations. And indeed, personal rituals can help soothe fears and ward off mental distress, as well as provide a sense of warmth and belonging. To illustrate what a powerful effect rituals have, consider a newly married couple with conflicting rituals when their first holiday season arrives. He says, "My family *always* opens presents on Christmas Eve, so we can't go to your parents' house until Christmas Day." She says, "Yes, but my whole family gets together on Christmas Eve for our big family dinner. It's always been this way, and I've never missed it. My parents will be so hurt if we aren't there." When rituals become associated with a sense of sameness and stability, any disruption of the ritual can feel like a threat, and you may react accordingly. In addition, attachment to a ritual can begin to overshadow the value that lies beneath the ritual, as with the young couple in this example, who run the risk of losing sight of the spirit of the holidays because each is attached to a well-established ritual.

Hank and Janice's Story

A young professional couple came to see me for a "problem" in their marriage. Hank, age twenty-seven, is an account executive, and Janice, age twenty-eight, is head of a prestigious fund-raising agency. When Janice called to make the appointment, she told me that their marriage was in serious crisis and that they really needed help getting through this difficulty. She said that she wanted to wait until our first visit to tell me what the problem was, as she was still very emotional about it.

During the first visit, Janice was visibly upset and Hank appeared embarrassed. They described themselves as driven people, and both had great aspirations for their professional and financial future. They both sat on several different community and civic boards and volunteered for many notable fund-raising efforts.

They shared how they had met in college at a fundraiser for the campus Young Republicans. They hit it off right away as they shared many interests, values, and beliefs. They both went on to become leaders in the local Republican Party and remain very active in it. Janice talked at length about how important this was to their position in the community and was obviously quite proud of it, mentioning many powerful and influential people they counted among their friends.

When the discussion came around to the crisis, Janice started crying and said she couldn't talk about it because of the shame it caused her. She asked Hank to tell the story. Looking sheepish, Hank reported that in a discussion the previous week, he'd told Janice that he didn't vote straight Republican in the last election—that he'd voted for a candidate of the Independent Party in one race because he strongly agreed with the candidate's positions on the issues.

As he told me that Janice had become irate, she broke in and exclaimed, "I can't even show my face at meetings now that I know this. What if people found out? For God's sake, Hank! I was president of the local party two years ago. Do you know what this will do to our reputation if it gets out? How could you do this to me? We have always been Republicans, and now you've gone and done this! I feel so betrayed."

Hank responded, "Well, at least I didn't vote Democrat."

It's amazing how much suffering this sort of attachment to the ritual of voting creates—how one small check mark in a single box, made in the privacy of a voting booth, can represent betrayal and a source of shame. This may seem like a tempest in a teapot, but attachment to concepts or beliefs can open rifts that grow wider with time.

ATTACHMENTS AND FEAR

As you now know, when your body is in its protective fight-or-flight state, your focus narrows so that you notice only what's relevant to the threat and your survival. So when you live in a chronic state of stress and SNS arousal, you don't have the opportunity to perceive much beyond what's relevant to the stress. Even if others give you great advice on how to change the situation, these possibilities won't seem valid or possible within your restricted awareness, so they may not make sense to you. It isn't that you're being difficult or resistant; you simply cannot see how those suggestions make sense in the context of your situation. When faced with that sort of conflict, it's all too typical to defend the illusions and delusions, rather than risk the discomfort of looking at things differently or changing.

The more you maintain your fear, the narrower your perspective becomes and the greater your attachments grow to be. A great metaphor for this is how lifeguards are taught how to approach person who may be drowning. People who are drowning are in a complete state of fear and commonly clutch onto a rescuer in a way that jeopardizes both people's safety. In the face of this intense fear, there's no reasoning with a drowning person; all the person sees is anything to grab to keep from drowning, even if doing so dooms any attempts at rescue.

Likewise, fear also drives mindless reactions in the emotional realm. If a husband discovers that his wife is having an affair, his focus is likely to narrow onto the cause of his pain and anguish. As a result, he may concentrate on blaming the other man and imagining how he'll take revenge, and may never look at why his wife was inclined to have an affair in the first place. His reaction is driven by the fear of losing his wife and his family, but it may actually hasten the likelihood that this will be the outcome, as his life and behaviors become increasingly out of control. Once again, creating the spaciousness that allows for clear seeing is the antidote. This allows you to develop an awareness of what's actually going on, what the situation calls for, and what resources are available to you, both internally and externally.

It's also important to remember that your reactions may not even have a bearing on the situation at hand. Big deal mind and the stories it spins can be powerfully convincing. To use a similar example, say the man in the preceding story had once had a girlfriend who cheated on him and this had been devastating to him. He may have formulated the story "Women can't be trusted. I can't let my guard down; I know I'll just get hurt again." As a result, he's always on the lookout for anything similar happening again. Not only is he attached to a story about what happened to him in the past and how devastating it was, he's also become stuck in a protective stance wherein he's constantly suspicious. If he continues to act and react on the basis of these stories, he may alienate his wife and destroy their relationship. His attachment to the story may become so strong that there's no way of talking him out of his suspicion that his wife is having an affair, even if she's not. The strength of attachments could skew his perspective so much that he may come to see his wife's attempts at reassuring him as proof that she's lying, and every demonstration of love as a further cover-up.

This is like the story of the little girl who was helping her mom fix the holiday ham. When her mom cut off the ends of the ham, the girl asked why she did that. Her mom replied, "It's something my mom always did. I think it makes the ham taste better." The girl promptly went off to ask her grandmother about the story behind the ham. Her grandmother said, "Oh, that's something *my* mom always did. I think it helps make the ham taste better." The girl went off to find her great-grandmother and ask her about the story behind the ham. Her great-grandmother laughed and said, "Oh, I had to cut the ends off the ham because when I was young I didn't have a pan big enough to fit the entire ham. I cut off the ends so the ham would fit into the pan." Because of the veils of illusion, delusion, and attachment surrounding this ritual, the women in this family couldn't even imagine cooking the ham differently when circumstances changed. The story—and the way things were done—stayed the same.

❧ PRACTICE: Discovering What You're Protecting ❧

In this practice, you'll apply clear seeing to how attachments maintain your illusions and delusions. As in some of the practices in chapters 4 and 5, you can use the theater technique to bring clear seeing to your attachments and any stories you've been living by that the attachments may serve to protect.

Assume the attitude of mindfulness. Breathe slowly, deeply, and gently, inhaling through your nose and exhaling through your mouth. Let all of your muscles relax—in your shoulders, face, jaw, neck, stomach, hands, and legs, let them all relax. Stay with awareness of your breath. Rest here for several minutes, then turn your attention inward.

Begin to look at your life as it is. Allow a particular event or situation in your life where things just aren't working to come into your awareness. Think of an area in your life that you find yourself protecting, consciously or unconsciously—perhaps attachments to stories about your partner, your children, your appearance, your career, or your abilities. As before, visualize carefully and gently holding this awareness in the palm of your hand.

As you patiently hold this concern in your awareness, begin to notice how important and solid it feels and why it persists. Specifically, what are you hanging on to that no longer brings about the results it once did or that doesn't yield the results you hope for. This may be a belief system (Women are always…; I'm never…; My husband is always…), a way of doing things (We've always done it this way; If it ain't broke, don't fix it), a behavior (smoking, drinking, not exercising, not calling loved ones), or a self-concept (I'm depressed, I'm not good at math, I'm blessed, I'm a Republican). Take some time to look at your attachment to maintaining the stories you've accepted in your life without having examined them closely and to see what happens when your attachment to these stories is threatened.

Remaining in this mindful space, take some time to consider and respond to the following questions.

As you allow yourself to explore this area with great patience and compassion, what does this attachment look like when your awareness is more open and spacious?

_____

_____

_____

_____

When something comes along that threatens to interfere with your attachment, how do you generally react? Do you perhaps turn to anger, blame, or avoidance?

_____

_____

_____

_____

_____

What do you notice about how your delusions and attachments interact? Pay particular attention to how they strengthen each other and how this may result in your concern feeling more solid, heavy, or serious.

_____

_____

_____

_____

As always, try to bring the lightness and curiosity of clear seeing to whatever you discover. This practice is designed to move you toward a deeper connection with the flow of your life. We all have attachments, and judging them as good or bad isn't the point. Rather, simply watch and notice how attachments may be playing a role in your suffering. As with illusion and delusion, clear seeing can help you gain perspective on your attachments so that you can just watch them without getting hooked by them. As you continue to practice viewing attachments in this way, they're likely to diminish and feel less compelling.

SUMMARY

The Buddha taught that attachment to conceptualizations and transient things is the root cause of suffering. All attempts to maintain a solid self by means of grasping and clinging to stories or fleeting objects are a form of attachment, and therefore a form of resistance to the natural flow of life. We cannot freeze our experience in space and time, and efforts to do so are doomed to fail. Even what each of us calls "self" is just an ever-changing phenomenon—and also part of the ongoing flow of the universe. The practices in this chapter have helped you identify your attachments and see the futility of attachment amidst the inevitable flow of life. While it is possible and worthwhile to work with attachment in isolation, all too often the chain reaction of illusion, delusion, and attachment proceeds so quickly that you may find yourself beset by aggressive impulses before you realize that attachment is a factor. So in the next chapter, we'll look at aggression, which is often your first signal that this chain reaction has occurred. By connecting with your pause and applying clear seeing, you can slow the chain reaction down and view the process without getting caught up in it, freeing you to choose more mindful responses to the situation at hand.

CHAPTER 7

Aggression

The final strategy of big deal mind is the veil of aggression. This isn't limited to violence and physical aggression; it can take on many other forms, including anger, blaming, shame, physical tension, resentment, jealousy, gloating, and defensiveness. Aggression represents the energy you put into keeping the veils of illusion, delusion, and attachment in place and is a consequence of solid self's attempts to control the flow of life events and restore a sense of safety and permanence. Unfortunately, turning to aggression to protect the other veils only serves to deepen our disconnection, leaving us increasingly isolated and ensconced in an anxious and reactive place.

That said, reacting aggressively is a normal aspect of the human condition that's hardwired into all of us. If you doubt this, just take the time to notice what happens when you point out to someone that she could be doing something a different way. It need not be something major, like how to stop smoking; it could be as trivial as cooking, fixing a faucet, arranging the furniture, or feeding the cat. You're likely to elicit an aggressive reaction (perhaps in the form of defensiveness). Although such suggestions seem harmless enough, they carry the implication that there's something defective or deficient in the other person's way of doing things. This feels like a threat and all too often draws forth the entire chain reaction of illusion, delusion, attachment, and aggression. As you can see, fear lurks beneath the aggression, and indeed, it has been said that anger is simply fear with a mask. Although this hardwired reaction to fear once served our survival, in the modern world it's frequently elicited by relatively minor, nonthreatening events.

There's nothing inherently wrong or bad about aggression and anger. They simply reflect a physiological and emotional reaction to fear and only become a problem when we act on them. This drains the joy from life and causes great suffering for ourselves and others. According to Buddhist monk Thich Nhat Hanh (2001), openly expressing aggression and anger, even just verbally, is counterproductive to the mindful spiritual path. Although you may think that expressing anger gets it out of your system, it actually feeds the seed of anger, causing it to grow and become stronger. Only understanding and compassion can neutralize anger.

WOUNDS THAT DON'T HEAL

At a retreat, I heard a little parable that really captures the downside of expressing anger and aggression. There was a little boy with a bad temper. His father gave him a bag of nails and told him that every time he felt angry, he should hammer a nail into the fence. The first day the boy drove thirty-seven nails into the fence. As the weeks passed, the number of nails he drove daily gradually decreased. Over time, the boy learned that it was easier to manage his anger and aggression than to drive those nails into the fence. The energy of his aggression was diminishing.

Eventually, a day came when the boy didn't feel any intense anger at all. He proudly told his father about it, and his father suggested that he now pull out one nail for each day that he was able to hold his temper. The months passed, and finally the boy was able to tell his father that all the nails were gone. His father took him by the hand and led him to the fence.

"You've done well, my son, but look at the holes in the fence. This fence will never be the same. When you say things in anger, they leave a scar just like these nail holes. If you put a knife in a man and draw it out, it won't matter how many times you say, 'I'm sorry.' The wound is still there."

AGGRESSION: THE FINAL RECOURSE

As the fourth veil, aggression is big deal mind's final recourse in the face of fear and perceived danger, a sort of "when all else fails" reaction. The fear reaction requires some sort of discharge, since your entire mind-body system is poised for a fight, flight, or freeze reaction. If illusion, delusion, and attachments haven't sufficed to explain away or neutralize the threat, on a very basic level you'll feel the urge to do something to protect your solid self.

Seeking this psychophysiological discharge requires that you view the situation or the other person as entirely separate from you, which creates a complete disconnection from the flow of your life. In this full-blown reaction mode, your sense of self is fully solidified, as is your sense of others and events. Someone or something must win, and someone or something else must lose. You may aggressively protect your physical self, or you may aggressively protect your thoughts, feelings, or beliefs. The more you react from aggression mind, the more your SNS is activated. The more you utilize the veil of aggression to protect your solid self, the more your veils of illusion, delusion, and attachment are intensified. This becomes a self-perpetuating downward spiral that prevents you from accessing patient, open, and compassionate responses.

ONE IS THE LONELINESS NUMBER

The truly distressing aspect of resorting to aggression is how very isolated and alone it can make you feel. Aggression mind is like quicksand: the more agitated and frenetic you get, the more you become entrapped in its fearful reactiveness. This state goes by many names—being stubborn, pigheaded, unreasonable, controlling, and so on—but in all cases it boils down to pitting your sense of solid self against the solid world.

If you remain in this closed-off, fearful state, you not only solidify your perception of the world as a dangerous place and continue to react accordingly, but you also solidify your sense of separateness. This is a very lonely place

Here's an example of how aggression mind operates. As you read through this example, notice how this individual moves through his illusion, delusion, and attachment minds, before his aggressive reaction finally emerges:

I was standing in line at the grocery store. The checkout person was an elderly woman who was trying to be careful about her work. The man in front of me was clearly impatient, and as time went on he started sighing deeply, shifting from foot to foot, and crossing and uncrossing his arms. Then he began mumbling derogatory comments about the clerk under his breath. Next, he turned to me and let loose with criticisms of her slowness, how the store shouldn't hire people like that, and what a pain in the ass the situation is for everyone. By the time it was his turn to check out, he was openly aggressive toward the clerk, telling her she should speed up, and when she handed him his receipt, he grabbed it from her and stormed out of the store. The more aggressive he became, the more disconnected and isolated he became from himself, the experience, and the checkout person.

When you're immersed in aggression mind, you can't be sensitive to your interactions and your experiences. You feel that events and people are separate from you and therefore a threat. Your body tightens and closes down, and your thoughts and feelings follow suit. As your thoughts and feelings narrow to fear-based reaction, you lose access to the patience, openness, and compassion required for mindful responses.

Have you ever noticed that when you resort to aggressive reactions, you continue to stew about the situation hours, days, or even years later? This how aggression mind solidifies your experience and keeps part of you stuck in the past, which keeps you from moving on and connecting with what's actually occurring. These aggressive reactions can also get stuck in the body, where they may show up in a myriad of physical symptoms, such as irritable bowel syndrome, low-back pain, ulcers, migraines, anxiety, and depression, to name just a few.

HOW TO WORK WITH AGGRESSION AND ANGER

There are two important techniques for working with anger: applying clear seeing and practicing patience. Clear seeing allows you to see aggression for what it is without getting caught up in it, and without opinions and judgments—about others, the situation, or yourself. Use your pause to find that space where you can see your aggression without acting on it. This doesn't mean you should try to suppress it, deny it, or get rid of it. In fact, these approaches are likely to intensify aggression. Instead, just give it plenty of space to run itself out and settle down, as in the rodeo story in chapter 2. If you use clear seeing and your pause in this way, you'll find that the aggressive energy gradually dissipates. Aggressive reactions are a process and as much a part of the flow of life as anything else. Though they feel very strong when they arise, with time they will subside. This is where practicing patience comes in. If you simply tune in to the natural flow of life events and allow yourself to move with them, you'll move on from the situation that elicited your aggression and find yourself in the next moment, which may offer something completely different.

❧ PRACTICE: Observing Your Aggression ❧

In this practice, you'll apply clear seeing and simply sit in the presence of your aggression so you can observe how it operates to maintain your suffering. Aggressive reactions can be important signposts in your journey as you work at responding to life more mindfully. It may be that only by noting an aggressive reaction will you realize that you've succumbed to illusion, delusion, and attachment. Not to worry; from this point you can work backward to better understand the other three veils and the roles they've played in the situation. Rather than judging yourself, just view aggression as a marker that allows you to shift toward clear seeing and a sense of spaciousness.

Assume the attitude of mindfulness. Breathe slowly, deeply, and gently, inhaling through your nose and exhaling through your mouth. Let all of your muscles relax—in your shoulders, face, jaw, neck, stomach, hands, and legs, let them all relax. Rest here for several minutes. Because this practice can call up difficult emotions, you may want to practice center point breathing during this time.

Bring your awareness to a situation where you employed aggressive actions to defend your solid self and illusions, delusions, or attachments. Take some time to visualize all of the details of that situation: where you were, the time of day, who else was around, and as much of the sensory information inherent in that experience as you can recall. This may be challenging, especially if you acted in ways that you now regret.

As in other practices in this part of the book, carefully and patiently hold this concern in your hand. After visualizing the situation in detail, bring clear seeing to it using the theater practice or whatever technique works best for you. If you find yourself becoming tense, defensive, or upset, simply return to your breath and a relaxed, open posture, then allow your awareness to drift inward once again.

After you've visualized the experience fully and spent some time there, take some time to contemplate and answer the following questions.

Explore the fear that drove your aggression in this specific incident. What was the fear? What was your big deal mind truly afraid of?

Explore the types of aggression you used. Was it verbal aggression, such as aggressive words, obscene language, name-calling, or using other demeaning terms? Did you turn to emotional aggression, like threats of withdrawal or abandonment, shaming, or guilt? Perhaps you were physically aggressive, whether that meant toward another person, inanimate objects, or yourself. Whatever form your aggression took, is that typical or atypical for you? Again, be honest with yourself.

If you were to let go of your illusion, delusion, attachment, and aggression, what would remain? Don't take refuge in pat answers; really look at this. If you let go of aggression mind or your attachment to a solid self, what would be left?

_____

_____

_____

_____

If you were to let go of your veil of aggression, what fear would this challenge you to face? Perhaps abandonment, ridicule, inadequacy, guilt, or imperfection?

_____

_____

_____

_____

This practice may have been painful, but it's crucial to recognize how the workings of aggression mind ultimately move you away from being connected to the flow of your life. Once again, don't judge yourself. Realize that this is the human condition, and that working with aggression is a struggle each of us faces. In fact, it may help if you repeat this practice and work with an incident when someone _else_ acted aggressively toward _you_. Visualize that incident in the same fullness, then answer all of the questions above, but this time try to imagine what illusions, delusions, and attachments may have fueled the other person's actions. Perhaps seeing the universality of this difficulty will help you find compassion for yourself, if that's what you need. Or perhaps it will help you find compassion for others and a way to respond to their aggression with equanimity.

PRACTICE: Detecting Early Signals of Aggressive Reactions

An important first step in transforming aggressive reactions into mindful responses is to notice the early signals that an aggressive reaction is building. Because they're ultimately the outcome of fear-based reactions and fear so profoundly affects the entire mind-body system, you can look for your own internal signposts that fear and aggression are present, in the form of both physical and emotional changes.

Assume the attitude of mindfulness. Connect with the rhythm of your breath and rest there comfortably for a few minutes.

Return to the situation you called to mind in the previous practice—a situation where you became aggressive in some way. Hold that situation in your awareness, again imagining it in as much detail as possible. Stay with this for a few minutes, bringing attention to how your body feels and what changes occur as you visualize the situation. Scan your entire body for physical responses, then remain in this mindful space as you take some time to contemplate and answer the following questions.

What do you notice about your body's responses? What muscles are tightening? Perhaps your jaw, back, stomach, or forehead? How has your breathing or heart rate changed? Do you feel flushed, hot, or sweaty, or perhaps cold and clammy?

As you continue to visualize the situation, shift your awareness to the emotions that arise. What do you notice about your emotions? For example, are you feeling anxiety, fear, agitation, aversion, distress, shame, or grief?

_____

_____

_____

_____

_____

Becoming familiar with the ways your body and emotions signal that an aggressive reaction is imminent can provide you with the chance to pause before reacting. That pause allows you to apply clear seeing to the situation and take a broader perspective. In this way, pausing breaks the chain reaction and gives you the opportunity to choose another response, rather than getting caught up in an automatic, fear-based, aggressive reaction.

PRACTICE: Using Aggression as Part of Your Mindful Path

Now that you've discovered some signals that you may be gearing up for an aggressive reaction, you can begin to apply patience, openness, and compassion to the chain reaction of illusion, delusion, attachment, and, ultimately, aggression. This allows you to bring more mindfulness to formerly difficult situations and find new ways of responding, in terms of not just actions, but also thoughts and feelings. To begin, use the same situation you've been exploring in the other practices in this chapter, and continue to visualize it through all three parts of this practice. As this process of slowing down and looking at your reactions becomes familiar, you can apply it to a wide variety of situations and difficulties in your life.

Patience

Recall the old adage to count to ten when you're angry. There's some powerful truth in this instruction. When you exercise patience and take the time to connect with your breath and your pause, you can short-circuit the chain reaction of illusion, delusion, and attachment before you find yourself in the grip of an aggressive reaction. When practicing patience in the face of aggressive reactions, adopt a spacious stance and allow the experience and your reactions to keep on moving.

Adopt the attitude of mindfulness, closing your eyes and resting comfortably for a few minutes. Let all of your muscles relax—in your shoulders, face, jaw, neck, stomach, hands, and legs, let them all relax. Practice center point breathing for a few minutes, finding the pause at the end of your out breath and resting there with each cycle of breath.

Bring the difficult situation you've been working with to mind again. Visualize it in full detail and notice how your aggressive reaction builds. As it builds, return to resting in your pause. Continue visualizing this difficult experience while also resting in your breath-and-pause cycle for a few minutes.

As you found your pause amidst a building aggressive reaction, what did you notice changing? How does your pause affect your aggressive reaction?

_____

_____

_____

_____

_____

Openness

Openness means accepting that all life is in constant motion and flow and maintaining a sense of curiosity about the outcome of any experience. It also means opening your senses to the flow of your life as it occurs—including fear-based reactions and aggression. Clear seeing is the key to remaining open amidst situations that have the potential for eliciting an aggressive reaction. It allows you to see the process by which aggressive reactions arise and how they can hook you into habitual protective strategies. As you simply watch this process with a sense of curiosity, you can begin to ask where all of this is coming from and what's likely to happen next, all without criticism or judgment.

Return to mindfulness awareness, reconnect with your breath, and rest here for a few minutes.

Bring the difficult situation you've been working with to mind again, visualizing it in full detail, and look at it through the lens of the theater practice. Imagine yourself in the theater, sitting all the way in the back, then allow the experience to begin to play out on the screen, picturing the people involved, yourself, the place, exactly what is occurring, how everyone is behaving, what is being said with words, and what's being said through tone of voice, body language, and facial expressions. Notice how in addition to the "you" up on the screen, there is also a "you" sitting near the front of the theater, who tends to get caught up in the action. Watch how the "you" on the screen behaves, then watch how the "you" in the front of the theater relates to what's occurring. Watch it all with a sense of wonder and curiosity, from a spacious place where you can observe how it all plays out and learn from what you observe.

When watching this experience play out while maintaining a sense of wonder and curiosity, what do you notice?

_____

_____

_____

_____

What happens to your aggressive reaction when the "you" at the back of the theater applies clear seeing and curiosity to the situation?

_____

_____

_____

_____

Compassion

One aspect of compassion is putting aside the need to manipulate and control outcomes and attuning to whatever is occurring with care and tenderness. A genuinely compassionate attitude doesn't change in reaction to any given person or situation and even extends to holding aggressive reactions and anger with tenderness. This stance opens the door to greater resonance with all beings and allows you to respond more gently to the events and people around you—and to yourself. As you hold aggression and anger in this practice, you'll come to understand that they're an expression of fear.

Return to mindfulness awareness, reconnect with your breath, and rest here for a few minutes.

Bring the difficult situation you've been working with to mind again, developing it in full detail. Notice all aspects of it and take a moment to connect with the fear beneath the aggression. What does your aggression serve to protect?

Now imagine that you're holding that fear, gently and compassionately, in the palm of your hand. If it helps, you can imagine it as a word, color, shape, animal, person, or any form that seems to fit. As you hold the fear, acknowledge it by simply naming it, without judgment or criticism. You don't even have to say what it is you're fearful about; just patiently and openly be in the presence of it.

As you continue holding this fear, reconnect with your breath, then practice center point breathing. Each time you return to your pause, offer your fear a statement that reflects your compassion, such as "While resting in my pause, I offer my fear compassion and permission to just be." Stay with this for three or four cycles of breath.

What happens to your aggression when you acknowledge the fear that lies beneath it?

_____

_____

_____

_____

As you gently hold this fear and offer it compassion, what happens to it?

_____

_____

_____

_____

_____

Use this practice in a variety of difficult situations where you find yourself inclined to respond with aggression. By repeatedly slowing the reaction process down and consciously applying patience, openness, and compassion, you'll break down old, habitual ways of reacting. You may feel that this practice is too time-consuming. This provides an excellent opportunity to apply patience! And although this practice is somewhat involved, it doesn't actually take that much time. In any event, you'll find that approaching difficult situations in this way is well worth the time you invest in it. Reacting with aggression can create so much discord and tension—in your relationships and even within yourself—that it can be enormously draining. As you develop your capacity to respond mindfully rather than reacting, you're likely to find that you have more energy, a greater sense of connection with others, and more ease and well-being in your life.

WORKING WITH THE FOUR VEILS

Watching the activity of the four veils will keep you from getting hooked into mindless reactions and go a long way toward deepening your mindfulness practice and your sense of presence throughout your life. Remember that mindfulness isn't about getting rid of the four veils; it's about bringing patient, open, and compassionate awareness to the flow of your life experiences and breaking the cycle of reacting.

What follows is a set of practices to employ over a four-week period. Each week you'll focus on a new practice aimed at helping strengthen mindfulness in the presence of one of the veils. If your mind resists or wanders as you engage in these practices, gently return to your breath and to repeating the statements below. Practice for about ten minutes as you begin and end your day.

Week 1: Illusion

During week 1, begin and end each day resting in the presence of your breath. As you breathe in, silently repeat to yourself, "I am reminded of my connection to all of life." As you breathe out, silently repeat to yourself, "I relax into the flow of all life."

Week 2: Delusion

During week 2, begin and end each day resting in the presence of your breath. As you breathe in, silently repeat to yourself "I will remain patient, open, and compassionate as my life unfolds." As you breathe out, silently repeat, "I will let go of the stories I tell myself."

Week 3: Attachment

During week 3, begin and end each day resting in the presence of your breath. As you breathe in, silently repeat, "I am letting go of resistance." As you breathe out, silently repeat, "I am embracing all that is offered in each moment."

Week 4: Aggression

During week 4, begin and end each day resting in the presence of your breath. As you breathe in, silently repeat, "I notice my fears and reactions." As you breathe out, silently repeat, "I strive to offer a patient, open, and compassionate response."

In addition to practicing as you begin and end your day, you can take these practices with you and use them throughout your day. If you begin to feel tense or stressed, return to your breath and silently repeat these reminders. If you're resisting the flow of life, use the practice for week 1. If you're caught up in listening to your stories about your life, use the practice for week 2. If you're being stubborn or otherwise attached, use the practice from week 3. And if you're feeling tight and reactive, use the practice for week 4.

If you continue to struggle with one or more of the veils, reread that chapter and focus on working with its practices. This is a process. The more you work with it, the more it will work in your life.

SUMMARY

As you navigate through the ongoing ebb and flow of your life experiences, take time to pause and reconnect with your awareness of how your veils of illusion, delusion, attachment, and aggression may be keeping you disconnected from others, from everything your life has to offer, and even from yourself. Through the difficult work of self-inquiry in part 2 of this book, you've come to understand yourself and your ways of responding to the world, creating a foundation you can build upon as you expand your practice out into the world around you. Part 3 of this book will help you apply mindfulness to everyday activities such as eating, walking, and driving—and to your awareness of the world around you. It will also help you bring patience, openness, and compassion to the more substantial challenges of mindfulness in relationships. In the final chapter, I'll introduce you to the ancient practice of loving-kindness meditation, which will help you extend compassion outward in an expansive way, ultimately to all living beings.

PART 3

Cultivating Mindfulness in All Aspects of Life

Cultivating spacious presence amidst your inner experiences is an important step toward creating a deep and profound connection to your larger life. In this final part of the book, you'll begin to apply what you've learned about fear-based reactions, solid self, big deal mind, and the four veils—and how to work with them—to create spaciousness in your daily life, in everything from eating, walking, and driving to relationships. You'll learn how to infuse spaciousness into everyday experiences that may have gone unnoticed as you moved through the routines of your life. You'll find that each experience in your daily life, no matter how seemingly mundane, offers an opportunity for mindfulness and mindful responses.

Although mindfulness isn't about rewards or specific outcomes, bringing spaciousness to your day-to-day activities will allow you to discover the beauty inherent in every moment of your life. And as you become increasingly present in your life and relationships, you'll learn how to express your true nature through every action and mindful response.

CHAPTER 8

Spaciousness in Daily Activities

Bringing spacious presence to some of the mundane activities of your daily life is valuable in many ways. One of the first things you'll notice is how often you go through your day mindlessly, on autopilot without being fully aware of whatever you're doing. This is how most people live much of the time. However, when you skim along the surface of life in this way, you can't experience all of the depth and richness available to you. The practices in this chapter will help you bring spacious presence to routine daily activities, inviting you to connect with yourself and your life in deep and meaningful ways. They will engage your entire mind-body system—because, after all, your mind and your body are partners in moving you through your daily life.

HABITS AND ROUTINES

Habits and routines have the effect of dampening your sensory awareness. Living on autopilot can feel easier, allowing you to go through your life with minimal disruption. However, these habits and routines are the root of mindless living, as they solidify the flow of your experiences so that you respond in preconceived ways that may not have any bearing on the current situation. Have you ever gone out to run errands and found yourself driving the route you take to work instead? There's actually a two-pronged type of mindlessness at work here. One aspect is being so caught up in thoughts or your internal world that you lose track of the current situation. The other aspect is how easily habitual, ingrained behaviors step in to fill the void when you aren't in touch with your present circumstances.

The next time your routine is disturbed, notice what happens. You're likely to find yourself resisting the change, griping, and complaining. For example, in a nearby town a bridge was recently taken out of commission for several months because it needed to be replaced. This caused a great stir among residents, as it required many of them to take a lengthy detour to get to work or school or to run errands. People complained about how much earlier they had to get up to get to work on time and having to navigate certain hills during the winter. Once the bridge reopened, however, many of these same people said that they were going to miss driving the detour, as it took them through some beautiful terrain. One person even decided he was going to take this route at least once a month, saying, "It makes me slow down and enjoy things more."

His comment offers great insight into how disrupting routines can awaken your awareness, allowing you to sense and observe in fresh new ways. Your eyes see things they hadn't noticed before, you feel the wind on your cheeks differently, and you hear sounds you had been screening out. Disruption of routines invites spaciousness into your life, making it easier to be present and alert. When you awaken your senses and cultivate spaciousness and connection in your everyday life, ordinary experiences become extraordinary. Each of your senses can provide an opening to knowing your world and your life without fear and rejection. Developing this awareness allows you to truly feel the miracle of your life.

SPACIOUS EATING

Eating provides an opportunity to bring spacious attention to an activity that you do every day, often without giving it much attention. In our fast-paced culture, eating is often viewed as an inconvenience—something to do quickly so that you can get back to doing whatever you were doing. As a result, many of us rely on fast food—and not just in the sense of convenience foods. For many people, the lunch hour isn't an hour; it may be no more than fifteen minutes, often spent eating at their desk or workplace or, all too often, in their car. Our eating culture could be summed up as "chew fast and swallow." Unfortunately, the tendency to swallow poorly chewed food only adds to the plethora of digestive disorders we experience, such as ulcers, irritable bowel syndrome, gastroesophageal reflux, and weight problems.

Consider this: It takes twenty minutes for a feeling of fullness in your stomach to be registered by the brain, which switches off the urge to eat—twenty minutes! Therefore, if you're eating rapidly, it's possible to consume a great deal of food between the time your stomach fills and the time it *feels* full. As a result, you'll end up feeling stuffed, and if you've eaten more than your body needs, much of the excess will be stored as fat.

Approaching eating with greater spaciousness allows you to slow down and savor an amount of food that's reasonable for your body. Ultimately, this will be more healthful, as well as more satisfying and genuinely nourishing.

✐ PRACTICE: Eating Mindfully ✐

Although you can practice mindful eating with any food, raisins are typically used to introduce this practice. So to get started and follow along with this practice, you'll need several raisins.

1. *Adopt the attitude of mindfulness.*

2. *Place several raisins in front of you and just sit and look at them. Choose one raisin that captures your attention, pick it up, and place it in the palm of your hand.*

3. *Describe what you see when you look at the raisin. It may feel odd, but I recommend stating your descriptions out loud throughout this practice. It will help foster mindfulness if you actually say—and hear—these descriptions of the things you normally don't notice.*

4. *Pick the raisin up, holding it between your thumb and index finger. Roll it around and describe what you notice about the raisin when you do this.*

5. *As you continue to roll the raisin around, turn your awareness to your hearing and listen to the raisin. Bring it up to your ear and really listen. How many times have you really listened to a raisin?*

6. *Smell the raisin and describe what you notice.*

7. *Bite the raisin in half. Position the half in your mouth on your tongue and hold it against the roof of your mouth. Describe what you notice.*

8. *Chew the raisin three times, then bring it back to your tongue and again hold it against the roof of your mouth. Describe what you notice.*

9. *Again, chew the raisin three times, then return it to your tongue and hold it to the roof of your mouth. What do you sense now?*

10. *Finally, finish eating the raisin.*

11. *Take some time to contemplate and answer the following questions.*

What did you notice about the raisin that you weren't aware of before?

_____

_____

_____

_____

You cultivated several experiences with the raisin before you actually sent it down to your stomach. What did you notice about how your body responded as you looked, touched, listened to, smelled, chewed, and swallowed the raisin?

_____

_____

_____

_____

What was it like to involve all of your senses in this practice?

_____

_____

_____

_____

How did this practice influence the way you relate to eating?

_____

_____

_____

_____

_____

What difference do you think will this make in the way you relate to eating in the future?

_____

_____

_____

_____

_____

Rest assured, I'm not advocating that you do this every time you eat—especially in restaurants! However, this practice does allow you to pay attention to what you're eating and decide if you like it. As an experiment, go buy a burger or some other junk food at one of the major fast-food chains. Take it home and try this practice with it. See how it really tastes when you take the time to genuinely experience the food you're putting in your mouth.

Another benefit of slowing down the eating process is giving the stomach a chance to signal the brain to stop eating. By slowing down, the full feeling has a chance to arrive at the brain before you overeat. When you nourish your body from a place of greater patience, openness, and compassion, you'll also have a better understanding of how food is involved in your reactions to the flow of your life experiences. If you have a problem with overeating or mindless or emotional eating, you can begin to see what events trigger that behavior and whether you're reacting to events in the outer world or internal events, such as feelings of boredom, anger, or stress. This awareness will allow you to turn off the automatic pilot that causes you to turn to eating as a way to cope.

Create a Spacious Eating Experience

Here are some suggestions on how you can approach eating with more mindfulness in your day-to-day life:

1. **Bring awareness to all of the activities surrounding eating.** Spacious eating includes being aware of all of the activities that relate to your relationship and experience with food and eating. This means everything from setting the table to clearing away the dishes after mealtime, including cooking and even selecting or purchasing your food. When you assume a careful, deliberate relationship with food, you enhance the way you approach your eating experience.

2. **Create an environment in which eating is the focus.** Minimize distractions such as television, telephones, computers, and reading. These distractions prevent you from devoting your attention to the spaciousness and presence required for mindful eating.

3. **Put a minimal amount of food on your plate.** You should be able to see the plate between your portions.

4. **Assume the attitude of mindfulness.** Sit in front of the food and just look at it, noticing everything you can as if you were an artist observing it for the first time. Become aware of the colors and smells. Take a moment to reflect on where the food came from: the person who prepared your meal, the store the food came from, the truck driver who hauled it from a warehouse to the store, the farmer who grew or raised the food, the farmer's family, and ultimately the rain, the sun, and the nutrients the food absorbed as it grew. All of that energy is right there in front of you. Those aren't just peas; they express everything that went into bringing them to your plate.

5. **Pause for a moment before you begin eating.** Return to your pause for several breaths. This will help reduce any activity of the sympathetic nervous system and promote activity of the parasympathetic nervous system, allowing you to begin the eating experience with a greater sense of spacious presence and respond to the food more mindfully.

6. **Choose which bite to have first.** Look carefully at that bite, then smell it before placing it in your mouth and beginning to chew. After taking the bite, put your utensil down and fold your hands in your lap. This will help break any tendency to eat mindlessly and repetitively. Sit patiently and chew the food, observing as many qualities of flavor and texture as possible. Throughout, maintain a

connection with your pause. If your mind wanders and begins reviewing the day or ruminating about what you'll be doing later, stop eating and return to your pause before you take another bite.

7. **Eat differently.** If you have the tendency to eat quickly, try eating differently. You can use your nondominant hand, eat while standing up, or eat with chopsticks. You can even try eating with your hands, as people in many other cultures do—though you may want to do this only in the privacy of your own home.

   Also, keep in mind that eating is an extremely sensual experience. Use all of your senses to embrace all aspects of the experience of nourishing your body.

- **See:** Look at what you eat. Really see the colors, textures, and shapes.

- **Smell:** Take in the aromas and, if there are several, sense how they interact.

- **Hear:** Listen to the sounds of the food as you prepare and consume it: the sizzle of sautéing, the bubbling of the soup as it boils, the crunching of a raw carrot as you chew.

- **Taste:** Beyond sweet, sour, salty, and bitter, foods have a remarkable array of flavors. Open your taste buds to the subtleties, and enhance your eating experience by using more herbs and spices to add nuances and depth of flavor.

- **Touch:** Feel the food as you prepare it, as you place it in your mouth, as you chew it, and as it travels down your esophagus and into your stomach.

SPACIOUS WALKING

Walking is another common, everyday activity that has a powerful potential to anchor you to your present experience. How often do you find yourself walking from one place to another so caught up in the machinations of big deal mind that you're virtually unaware of your surroundings? By practicing mindful walking and then extending this practice into your day-to-day life, you can move through your life with greater awareness and a deeper sense of patience, openness, and compassion. If you adjust the pace at which you walk, your movement will begin to reflect your response to your life, not a reaction to it. You'll move through your life at your pace and not the pace dictated by external events.

Change Your Pace

Walking mindfully can be as simple as connecting with your senses and deliberately changing the pace at which you move through your world. When you were an infant learning to walk, you were exceptionally aware of your experience of walking. Just trying to get yourself upright required full physical effort and your total visual attention. Once upright, you focused every ounce of concentration on moving each foot out in front of the other. All of your senses were alert and attuned to the activity at hand.

Once you mastered walking, it no longer required that type of attention. You got to where you could walk and push something, walk and talk, walk and look for something, and perhaps you have arrived at a point where you can walk and eat at the same time—maybe while talking on your cell phone! Your attention to the walking process has receded into the background, and you may view it as simply something you do in order to get somewhere and accomplish something else. If you're like most people, walking has probably became automatic and mindless.

❧ PRACTICE: Walking Mindfully ❧

This practice involves walking more slowly and deliberately than is normal in our culture, so you may feel self-conscious at first. I recommend that you begin your mindful walking practice in a fairly private place, such as your home or yard or an uncrowded park. Wherever you practice, it's best to ensure there will be minimal distractions so you can focus on your walking experience.

Adopt the attitude of mindfulness, standing with your knees slightly bent and your feet shoulder width apart. Soften your gaze to see whatever is in your field of vision without looking at anything in particular. See without looking. You can accomplish this by looking at the ground about ten feet ahead of you. Rest here for a few minutes, connecting with your pause.

Begin walking at a normal pace.

Start to slow the pace down just a bit—nothing too dramatic or sudden. Slowing down too much too quickly may create a problem with balance and distract you from the experience of walking.

Once you've found a comfortable slower pace, connect with any of your senses. You might say to yourself, "As I walk, I notice everything that comes into my visual awareness" or "As I walk, I become aware of whatever I hear" or "As I walk, I notice everything I feel physically." If physical sensations seem tricky or difficult to focus on, think of the wind on your face, the sun on your neck, your feet in your shoes, and so on. Depending on the environment you're in, you may be able to bring your awareness to smells, as well. Taste would be pretty tricky here, so reserve that sense for mindful eating.

As with all other mindfulness practices, becoming distracted is normal. When this happens, just gently bring your awareness back to your pace and your senses.

Continue walking slowly and mindfully for about fifteen minutes, then take some time to contemplate and answer the following questions.

What did you notice as you slowed your pace?

_____

_____

_____

_____

_____

What sense or senses did you connect to? What did you notice through these senses as your pace slowed?

_____

_____

_____

_____

_____

What awareness did you have about the pace at which you normally move and the pace you adopted for this practice? How was your body feeling? What changes occurred?

_____

_____

_____

_____

_____

Continue practicing mindful walking regularly. For example, as you finish your day at work or school, pause a moment, adopt the attitude of mindfulness, and change your pace as you walk away. You can also do this when you're walking through the grocery store, down the sidewalk, in a park, or just about anywhere. There are endless opportunities to develop a mindful connection to walking, so as this practice becomes familiar, begin to widen your practice by walking in different environments.

Another benefit of this practice is that it can help you find the pace that's right for you—not just in walking, but throughout your life. As you adjust your automatic, habitual pace and invite your senses to awaken, you'll find that your responses to whatever you encounter will become infused with greater patience, openness, and compassion.

Alice's Story

Alice came to me for therapy to help in coping with the stresses in her life. She was in her midthirties and a single mother of four boys, ages four to thirteen, three of them diagnosed with attention-deficit/hyperactivity disorder. She worked as a nurse, and fortunately her mother was able to help with the boys on the days when she worked. As Alice opened up about her situation and her feelings, I noticed that she referred to herself as never being able to find her pace and that she used the word "pace" frequently.

"I never get the chance to wake up at my own pace. What usually wakes me up is my kids jumping on my bed, arguing in the bathroom, or having a cereal fight in the kitchen. Once I'm up, I have to rush around to get things done around the house before I go to work. The pace at work is terrible. From the moment I get on the floor, there's always something that requires my immediate attention. I can't even take a minute to get a cup of coffee. By the end of the day I'm exhausted, and also feeling guilty that I haven't seen my kids. So I hurry to my mom's to pick them up and rush home to have some quality time with them. They're usually pretty wound up—and clamoring for my attention. As you can imagine, the pace at home is wild. Once all of the boys are in bed and I finally have a moment to myself, I usually just veg out in front of the TV, have a couple of beers, and eventually fall asleep. All week it's the same, then weekends are taken up with soccer games, basketball games, housework, visiting my mom, and doing laundry. I haven't found my own pace. I'm always rushing around at everyone else's pace or to do things for other people."

Notice all the words Alice used to describe the pace at which her life operated. I asked her if she'd be interested in discovering what her true pace was. She responded, "Yeah, right. Like that's going to happen!"

"Well," I said, "we still have forty minutes remaining in our session. Would you be interested in trying something that might help you find your pace?" Reluctantly, she agreed.

We went into a large room next door to my office where I conduct classes and seminars. I keep a metronome in that room precisely for the purpose of helping people find their pace. I asked Alice to stand about three to four feet behind me, then I set the metronome at a speed that translates to a mildly brisk pace. I asked Alice to follow me as I walked around the room, taking a step for each click of the metronome. We walked around the room several times at this pace, then each time we passed the metronome, I slowed it down a click. After a couple more circuits around the room, I moved out of the way and asked Alice to continue and said I'd follow her. I also asked her to do as I had done, slowing the metronome down each time we passed it until she found a pace that was comfortable for her.

After three more passes she stopped and began to cry. She said, "Tom, I have to sit down." As we sat, she sobbed and finally said, "I have never felt what it's like to move at my pace. I think I felt for the first time how my body feels when I'm walking at my own pace. This was wonderful!"

On her way home, Alice stopped by a music store and bought herself a metronome. She said that she now wakes up twenty minutes earlier, before the boys get up, goes to her basement, sets the metronome, and walks at her own pace. "At least I can start my day at my own pace," she said. With time, she started doing the same thing at night, just before going to bed.

Slowing down her pace allowed her to experience firsthand what her pace was in many other areas of her life. As Alice practiced claiming her pace at home, she became aware of how she could influence her pace at work. Taking breaks, walking down to the cafeteria, and walking to and from her car all became chances for her to interrupt her old pattern of racing around, unaware of the effects her rushed pace had on her physical and emotional well-being. One night when she found herself bolting down her dinner mindlessly, she paused a moment and then began reciting the rhythm of her metronome in her mind to help her slow down and tune in to eating. Overall, she reported having more energy and subsequently more patience both at work and at home.

⟪ PRACTICE: Walking Through the World of Distractions ⟫

Walking mindfully in a quiet, serene place is usually fairly easy, as there are fewer external distractions to engage big deal mind. Taking mindful walking into busy environments presents a greater challenge. This practice will give you the opportunity to feel how mindfully modifying your pace affects the way you experience moving through the world of distraction. This practice is similar to the practice in chapter 4 where you visited a mall or other busy location and spent some time taking in information from all of your senses. This time, you'll practice mindful walking in a similar environment. This can be challenging, so be sure you're comfortable with mindful walking in a less stimulating environment before you try this.

Go to the mall or any similar busy location, such as a grocery store, train station, or sidewalk. Find a place where you can take a few moments to adopt the attitude of mindfulness, softening your gaze to see whatever is in your field of vision without looking at anything in particular. You can accomplish this by looking at the ground about ten feet ahead of you. Stay with this for a few moments but not too long, or people might start getting nervous.

Begin walking at a slower pace than you normally would, remaining mindful and continuing to see without looking.

Notice everything that pulls on your attention: visual stimuli ("Oh, look, a big sale"), sounds (music from a teen clothing store), smells ("Mmm, cinnamon rolls"), thoughts ("Need to pick up some milk on the way home"), and so on.

Each time your sense of spaciousness begins to close down around something specific (feeling self-conscious, noticing a sale, smelling food or coffee, the chatter of a distracted mind, overhearing a conversation, focusing on an attractive person), slow your pace down for a moment, return to your pause, and soften your gaze, then resume your spacious walking.

Continue walking in this way for about ten minutes, then take some time to contemplate and answer the following questions.

What did you notice as you walked at a slower-than-normal pace? Did you become more aware of your environment than you otherwise might have? If so how?

_____

_____

_____

_____

What sense or senses did you connect to? What did you notice through these senses as you adopted a slower pace? How did your awareness shift? Did colors seem different? Did you hear things you normally might not hear?

_____

_____

_____

_____

What awareness did you have about the pace at which you normally move and the pace you adopted for this practice? How was your body feeling? What changes occurred?

_____

_____

_____

_____

Mindful walking can be a powerful way to connect with beginner's mind, or seeing without preconceptions—something that was remarkably evident when I conducted this practice at a daylong mindfulness seminar in Manhattan. I gave the participants the above instructions and asked them to go out into Times Square to do their mindfulness walk. When they returned, we discussed what their experience was like. There were typical responses: "I felt a bit self-conscious at first," "I noticed that my breathing relaxed," I began looking at people more," "I noticed that my shoulders relaxed," "I noticed how incredibly noisy it is out there!" Then a man in his early thirties said, "I've lived in Manhattan all my life. As a kid, every day I walked through Times Square on my way to school. During this practice, I became truly aware of Times Square for the very first time. Thank you!"

As you develop your own mindful walking practice, you'll find that you reconnect with familiar surroundings in new and deeper ways. Your experience will be richer as the world around you becomes more engaging and alive. As you begin to practice in places that are more public, you may struggle with feeling self-conscious. This too is grist for the mindfulness mill. You can use it as an opportunity to simply be mindful of your internal experience without identifying with it or becoming attached to it.

SPACIOUS DRIVING

Driving can be very stressful, but it also presents a tremendous opportunity for developing careful, mindful responses and can even become a kind of meditation practice in its own right (Boorstein 2006). Here are a few suggestions for ways that you can use driving as a meditation.

Switch off the radio and experience the silence. We often drive while listening to the radio, other music, or audio books. Just as an experiment, try seeing what it's like to drive without these added sounds. At first it might seem as if something is missing, but the quiet can invite you to return to your pause. You're likely to find that the silence gives you an opportunity to fill your awareness with other perceptions, which you may find more enriching.

Pay attention. If you aren't listening to the radio, you can notice other things. Look for any tension in your body, such as a knot in your belly, your hands gripping the steering wheel too tightly, or a clenched jaw. The quiet can also create more space for you to feel the texture of the road beneath your wheels or the air against your face. As you bring spaciousness to your driving experience, you'll become more aware of your internal state, including the SNS arousal that's often elicited by driving. Returning to your pause will help activate your parasympathetic nervous system and rebalance your internal state. Notice how this practice helps you become more patient, open, and compassionate, where you might once have been impatient, frustrated, or angry.

Slow down. As an experiment, try driving at or just below the speed limit. Most of us tend to want to push the speed limit, driving just a little faster than allowed. Driving just a fraction under the speed limit can take away a lot of tension. Move over into the slower lane if necessary. Also, when driving on longer stretches of road, try putting your car on cruise control. Notice if you react to driving at a steady rate of speed.

Notice your attitude. Often we become competitive or judgmental while driving, and this definitely leads to tension. Big deal mind can become extremely attached to such trivialities as your place in traffic or that last parking space, a mind-set that transforms other drivers into threats and causes you to react mindlessly. Rather than succumbing to road rage, expand your awareness to experience traffic as a flow and to see yourself as simply part of that flow. Make a practice of noticing cars trying to enter the road, and adjust your speed to let them in if it's safe to do so. Notice if you're in a hurry and how that makes you feel. How does it feel if you let your pace slacken a little?

As drivers pass you, wish them well. In chapter 11, I'll discuss loving-kindness in depth. As a warm-up of sorts, you can begin by extending well-wishes to other drivers. Simply say, "May you be well. May you be happy." You can say these phrases out loud or just in your mind. (Unfortunately, it may be best to not say them directly to other drivers.) You can offer these well-wishes anytime, but it's especially beneficial to do so whenever other people's driving irritates or angers you. Remember that you don't know what they're dealing with. Maybe they've just been fired, or perhaps they're thinking about a loved one who's seriously ill or dying.

Use every stoplight to practice greater mindfulness. When you've stopped, it's safe to let your awareness more fully connect with your breathing. Notice how your body feels, and release any tension you may feel in your neck, jaw, hands, shoulders, or anywhere else. You can also take the time to notice what's around you: the sky, the land, the plants, the buildings, other cars, and other people. Take that moment to wish those other people well. Also try thanking the stoplight for this opportunity to pause and reconnect.

Sit for a moment and take three deep breaths. As you get into your car to start on your journey and after you've arrived at your destination, take a moment to just sit and breathe slowly and deeply. Connect with your pause and notice whether and to what extent your fear-based SNS has been activated. Many aspects of driving naturally activate the SNS, since you need to be alert and react quickly. Reconnecting with your pause at the beginning, during, and at the end of your trip will keep your SNS from becoming overstimulated and therefore overly reactive. This is an effective tool to use to ward off road rage.

Take a different route. If you routinely drive to a certain destination by taking the same route, try something different. Go through another neighborhood and notice the houses, gardens, and activity in the neighborhood. Or go through another part of town and notice the buildings, the businesses, and the people. If possible, take a detour through a park or a more rural area and notice how you feel once you arrive at your destination.

Remembering the Flow

A major benefit of practicing spacious driving is increasing your awareness of life as a flow. Driving is definitely a flow experience as you and the drivers all around you merge into the ongoing stream of traffic. Allowing yourself to become an active part of the flow without imposing your fear-based illusions, delusions, attachments, and aggressions onto that flow is a truly mindful practice, and one that's all too rare in our culture. When you practice driving in this way, notice how you feel when you arrive at your destination.

The flow of traffic is a wonderful metaphor for the flow of life. As you translate your experiences in mindful driving into other aspects of your life, resisting impatience, willfulness, and aggression, you'll find that the journey becomes more enjoyable. You'll broaden your spacious connection to the flow of life and begin to see every experience of your life as an opportunity to express mindful responsiveness.

FINDING THE PAUSE IN DAILY ACTIVITIES

I first discussed the pause when I introduced center point breathing. A similar pause occurs as you complete each task and, indeed, each between each step in any task throughout your day.

Take the time to observe a brief spacious pause at the end of each aspect of your activity, and notice how this allows you to bring mindful attention to the actual event. Your movements will take on a quality of care and even grace. As you approach daily tasks in this way, bring your awareness to what you see, hear, smell, and feel—both in a tactile sense and internally. Embracing the natural pauses in any activity prevents you from being distracted by big deal mind and allows you to remain connected to the beauty and richness available to your senses at all times. In this way, the pause becomes an integral component of clear seeing.

Throughout your day, every day, take time and bring clear seeing to these pauses so your senses can reconnect with what's actually going on. Moving mindlessly between activities frequently shows up as forgetting, dropping, or knocking things over, spilling things, tripping, and the like. When this happens, don't berate or judge yourself. Simply view these mishaps as an invitation to look for the pauses available in the flow of your experience.

There is an ancient saying: "Before enlightenment, chop wood, carry water. After enlightenment, chop wood, carry water." It speaks to how bringing spacious awareness to even the most mundane tasks invites a deeper sense of connection to your experiences. In fact, these mundane experiences are an essential part of your mindfulness path. The next thing you do, the next thing you say, or the next experience that unfolds—these have everything needed to bring you closer to a deeper, more meaningful, and more mindful connection.

Really endeavor to keep from rushing from one activity to another. Pause between each bite of food at mealtime. Pause for a moment before you turn on the ignition of your car. Pause before you answer the phone. A red light in traffic is a wonderful gift in driving, inviting you to pause mindfully. Explore all of the places in the flow of your life where you can take a brief, mindful pause. Connecting with these pauses helps bring forth a profound understanding of just how transitory your experiences are. As you transition through these pauses, you can see how a particular event arises, occurs, and recedes. Each event is an experience in itself, not something to rush through on the way to something else.

SUMMARY

In this chapter, you've practiced mindful eating, walking, and possibly driving, and have started to look for the inherent pauses in daily activities that will invite spaciousness, richness, and depth into your life. Awareness of the pause heightens your ability to respond mindfully and carefully as you go through your day-to-day activities. Building on the foundation you've established using the practices in this chapter, the next chapter will introduce you to haiku awareness as a way to help you extend your connection to your pause and bring mindful responses to all of the moments of your life.

CHAPTER 9

Haiku Awareness

This chapter will expand on the practices you learned in the previous chapter by introducing you to haiku awareness, a way of looking at the world that you can use to mindfully connect with all of your experience, many times throughout your day. Yes, haiku is a style of poetry. And no, you don't have to like poetry to benefit from this approach, nor are you required to become a poet. However, even if you aren't into poetry, I think you'll enjoy working with haiku. Most people do. Plus, haiku is a perfect complement to mindfulness, being based on the fundamental themes of spaciousness and awareness. The beauty of haiku awareness is that it isn't something you have to work at creating. Any haiku you craft is a reflection of your awareness; it's right there in your presence, just waiting to be noticed.

LANGUAGE, COMMUNICATION, AND SPACIOUS AWARENESS

In Japanese, *hai* means "joke, fun, or unusual," and *ku* mean means "sky, emptiness, or the void." Haiku is also referred to as a playful verse, and learning how to use haiku will definitely introduce a sense of playfulness into your mindfulness practice.

You might wonder how haiku is relevant to the experience of mindfulness. Haiku is more than a form of poetry; it's a way of observing your world and your experience in it. It isn't about trying to discover totally new things; it's about perceiving things in a totally new way (Spiess 2002). Just as wood is consumed in a fire, the words in haiku are consumed in the process of creating the experience to which the words refer. It's a powerful approach to creating the awe and wonder of beginner's mind.

Writing haiku is a process of utilizing a small number of words to promote an intimate connection with your direct experience. In haiku, each word resonates with the emotional power of a sentence or even a paragraph. To that end, here are a few pointers to keep in mind to make the most of your haiku experience:

- Write your haiku in three lines, the first line comprising five syllables; the second, seven syllables; and the third, five syllables. However, do note that the 5-7-5 rule works well in Japanese but isn't quite so fitting for English, so don't get sidetracked by trying to strictly adhere to this rule. If your haiku is 4-6-5, 3-8-4, or even 6-6-3, this is close enough. The point isn't the number of syllables; it's taking the time to pause, awaken, and capture the experience that's occurring.

- Don't make reference to yourself or other people. Leave out *I, we, you, he, she,* and *they.* Just capture the details of your experience.

- Don't make judgments. Doing so imposes your big deal mind onto this process. Leave out what you think and feel. Create enough spaciousness to invite others to fill in the space with their own thoughts and feelings.

Let's look at a couple of examples so that you can see the difference the first two guidelines make. Here's a winter haiku that doesn't observe the first two rules:

> Walking to my car
> The winter wind howling
> I hate winter!

The personal references and judgments may be true, but they detract from the experience and disconnect you from the flow of the experience. Here's an example of how that same haiku might be revised to follow the first two guidelines:

Approaching the car
The winter wind howling
Will it start?

This allows both the person writing and the reader to have their *own* experience. Also notice that the syllable count in this haiku is 5-6-3. That's okay.

As you can see, the very nature of haiku is spaciousness. Writing haiku challenges you to distill your experience into three simple lines that capture the object of your spacious awareness. Its unadorned approach to language leaves space for readers to feel their own responses. The words point to the space, and readers fill in their responses. Haiku doesn't tell you what to feel; rather, it invites you to access your own experience in regard to whatever the haiku points to. Haiku allows you to experience each moment with a freshness and newness that opens the door to spacious responses, in other words, to beginner's mind.

Here are some examples of how haiku captures the spacious quality of each moment, allowing readers to experience their unique response to the verses. After reading each one, pause and allow your responses to emerge. These responses may take the form of memories, feelings, images, or sensations. Avoid expecting anything. Remember, this is a practice of creating spaciousness in any given moment. Just be with what is and allow your responses to emerge.

Clutter of the past
Memories float by
On the mist of low clouds

The sky is bluer
Streams run like adolescents
Sweet mountain fragrance

Ant travels along
The grain of wood tells its story
Of many years past

HAIKU AND BEGINNER'S MIND

As you learn to apply haiku to expanding your sense of spacious experience in life, you'll have another tool to minimize the effects of the four veils and instead embrace clear seeing. At this point, don't worry about learning haiku as a technique; just welcome it as an awakening to the simplicity and beauty of your experience that allows you to mindfully respond to what presents itself to your senses. Your senses are truly the gateway to connecting with the flow of your life, and embracing haiku moments helps maintain that all-important connection. Ceasing activity to construct haiku enhances your connection with the flow of what is actually going on and helps you observe more of the natural pauses that are ever-present in the unfolding of your experience.

CREATING HAIKU AWARENESS

In addition to the guidelines above, an important pointer on crafting your own haiku is that the subject matter for each line should reflect an important aspect of your view of your world. Make sure the words reflect your way of looking at your world. Relax and be creative. Especially at first, don't be concerned with doing it "right"; just play with observing and write the words that capture your observation. The more you work on crafting haiku, the more you'll appreciate that there's no urgency. Just as Michelangelo looked at a piece of granite and saw the sculpture waiting to be freed, you will become comfortable seeing each moment as a haiku waiting to be noticed.

Poet and editor Lonnie DuPont (2001) has systematized a method for learning to write haiku:

1. Read haiku.

2. Find a haiku moment.

3. Find a haiku place.

4. Express your observation in three lines.

I've divided this process into two practices. The first involves Lonnie DuPont's first step: reading haiku. The second experience will be informed by the remaining three steps as I guide you in writing your own haiku.

✎ PRACTICE: Heightening Awareness by Reading Haiku ✎

This practice gives you an opportunity to read and reflect upon haiku. As you read haiku, don't necessarily view it as poetry; see it as an avenue of awareness, observation, and connection. Be open, use clear seeing, and allow yourself to reflect upon the trickles of awareness that the haiku drips into your mind. As you read haiku, observe how it draws your awareness into the true essence of the experience it speaks to. Don't rush through reading haiku; it isn't like reading a book. After reading a haiku, pause with it and let it percolate, resonate, frustrate, or intimidate…and start the spark of observation and awareness.

Take time with each of the following haiku. Experiment with connecting with your pause, then reading through the haiku in that pause. After reading each haiku, pause and answer the question beneath.

Tapping on the roof
The gutters, the sidewalk
A gentle rain falls

As you rest in your pause and recite this haiku, what comes into your awareness, in terms of thoughts, feelings, and memories?

_____

_____

_____

_____

As the dawn
Pulls back the blanket of night
A Robin sings

As you rest in your pause and recite this haiku, what comes into your awareness, in terms of thoughts, feelings, and memories?

_____

_____

_____

_____

Coffee cup
Resting on the table
Morning light dances

As you rest in your pause and recite this haiku, what comes into your awareness, in terms of thoughts, feelings, and memories?

_____

_____

_____

_____

Morning sun peeking
Excited leaves fluttering
A bird's lonely song

As you rest in your pause and recite this haiku, what comes into your awareness, in terms of thoughts, feelings, and memories?

_____

_____

_____

_____

I once heard a story that legendary trumpeter Miles Davis advocated not playing what *is* there, but rather, playing what *isn't* there. Haiku is similar. The words aren't really what carries the ability to expand awareness; that power lies in what the words point to. Notice where the words in each of the haiku above pointed for you.

You might like to expand this practice by looking for haiku online or at your library. Take the same spacious approach to poems by people from different times and different cultures and notice what they bring to your awareness. When reading any haiku, remember that the words are pointing you in a direction that invites a deeper exploration of your unique experiences and responses.

WRITING HAIKU

Now let's take a closer look at the process of writing haiku in light of the remaining three steps outlined by Lonnie DuPont: finding a haiku moment, finding a haiku place, and expressing your observation in three lines.

The haiku moment is when you adjust your awareness to become connected with the flow of experience and the emotions (both yours and the reader's) that can be brought to this experience. Accept that your expression will be brief and simple. Remember that the haiku will be a finger pointing at the moon; don't get lost looking at the finger and miss observing the moon. Also, remember that every moment is a potential haiku moment, so you aren't in search of a certain type of situation, you're simply choosing to apply your haiku awareness.

As with a haiku moment, there are no criteria for a haiku place; any place can be a haiku place. The key to finding a haiku place is having a keen awareness of the environment around you. Although a natural environment is a traditional focus in haiku, as you develop haiku awareness you'll begin to see how you can apply this to any place and any activity you're engaged with, from your bedroom or the kitchen, to traffic or a parking lot, to your office or an elevator. The haiku place is wherever you are when you pause and awaken to your experience as it occurs. The point of haiku awareness is to reconnect with your pause, and this pause is inherent in each moment, no matter where you are. Pause and connect with your senses.

❧ PRACTICE: Writing Your Own Haiku ❧

Having found a haiku moment and place (or having had a haiku moment and place find you!), you're ready to craft your haiku.

Express your observations in three lines. Again, don't be fixated on the 5-7-5 syllable count, though you might want to aim for an overall count of about 17 syllables. Make each word count. Focus on using sensory-rich language that evokes images with as few words as possible. Have each line carry a specific image or observation from your current experience. Stay away from memories. They will only disconnect you from your immediate experience. If you find yourself at a loss, take a walk and periodically stop and notice aspects of where you are in that very moment. Let that be the focus of each line. Haiku awareness must arise from real-life experiences.

As you're getting started, you may feel a need for more guidance. Here are a few examples of how you might structure your haiku.

Line one: Where?   Walking in the field
Line two: What?   A squirrel scampers away
Line three: When?   Early morning frost

Line one: Sight   Peach-colored sky
Line two: Tactile sensation   Brisk breeze blowing
Line three: Smell   Fresh autumn fragrance

Line one: Tree   The old oak stands
Line two: Color   Naked against the gray sky
Line three: Water   A dewdrop forms

If you want *really* specific guidance, try the following approach using the table below. Take a word from column 1, then a word from column 2, and combine them to make your first line. Next take a word or phrase from each of the next three columns (columns 3 through 5) and combine them to make your second line. Finally take a word from column 6, then a word or phrase from column 7 and combine them to make the third line. Here's an example from the words in the table:

Strange mountain
Floating against the snow
Rain pauses

Notice that the haiku doesn't necessarily make sense in a logical fashion, yet it evokes a response. Pay attention to this response, as it is what connects you to the spacious quality of each of your present moments.

1	2	3	4	5	6	7
Little	butterfly	Floating	over	the flowers	Spring	is beginning
Strange	flower	Playing	against	the tree	Summer	is over
Bright	mountain	Always	upon	the snow	Fall	moment
Yellow	leaves	Growing	behind	the water	Winter	fragrance
Red	moon	Stands	with	the sky	Nighttime	coming
White	sun	Looking	amidst	the wind	Morning	breeze
Lost	fog	Resting	through	the road	Cold	dream
Quiet	lake	Reaching	without	the mist	Dawn	starts
Hopeful	cloud	Running	away	the valley	Rain	pauses
Restless	seed	Exploring	toward	the hill	Birdsong	arrives

Take some time to create haikus from this table and see how you respond to each. Writing haiku in this way isn't in the true spirit of constructing a haiku, but it does give you a feel for the form and also allows you to begin to experience how this spartan use of words can elicit a deep response. Keep playing with this, using different combinations each time and noticing how different combinations of words elicit different responses. You can write your practice haiku here:

Once you get the hang of it and become comfortable with using just a few words to capture the essence of a moment, you can start to write haiku about your actual experiences. For example, the next time you're stopped at a traffic light, you could let your awareness construct a little haiku—three lines, each depicting some aspect of your awareness, like this:

> Motor humming
> Feet resting on the floor
> Waiting

Or the next time you're waiting in line at the grocery store, connect with your haiku awareness and construct a three-line vignette that evokes the scene, like this:

> Hands on the basket
> Child's red face screaming
> National Enquirer

As you explore haiku awareness, you'll begin to notice how it invites you to shift from reacting to responding.

Take a moment now to put this book down and allow your awareness to absorb aspects of your present experience, then capture the essence of that awareness in three lines. You can write your haiku here:

_____

_____

_____

_____

Now pause for a moment, then take some time to contemplate and answer the following questions.

What do you notice now, after writing your haiku? What sort of changes did this practice bring about in each of your senses?

_____

_____

_____

_____

Did you notice any physical changes, perhaps in muscle tightness, breathing, heart rate, or posture?

_____

_____

_____

_____

To get a feel for how connecting with haiku moments can help you remain connected to the flow of your life, repeat this practice.

> *Put down this book and once again allow your senses to absorb aspects of your experiences in this very moment, then capture the essence of that awareness in three lines. You can write your new haiku here:*

_____

_____

_____

Several moments passed between writing your two haiku. How does the second haiku reflect the changes in your experience?

_____

_____

_____

_____

What new awarenesses emerged in this haiku that weren't present in the first one? Was this one perhaps more visual, tactile, or auditory?

_____

_____

_____

_____

List several places where you typically find yourself resisting your experience because some aspect of it is unpleasant to you, perhaps work, traffic, cooking dinner, washing the dishes, mowing the lawn, listening to your three-year-old talk (and talk and talk and talk), hearing your teenager's music blaring from his room, and so on.

_____

_____

_____

_____

Practice approaching these situations with haiku awareness, and then actually write your haikus down somewhere. Try connecting with your breath and your pause, then simply begin to notice your experience in the haiku way. After you've done this a few times, return to this page and write about how your haiku awareness affected your experience.

As you can see, haiku doesn't freeze or solidify experiences; it allows you to pause and take notice of whatever is unfolding. Pause again a few moments later and you'll connect with another experience of what is unfolding. Haiku is a fun and yet profound approach to removing the veils, avoiding a sense of separateness, and connecting with the pause in order to invite beginner's mind and clear seeing into your experiences. Pausing to create haiku awareness allows you to pay attention to the inherent richness and beauty in your life and respond to the dynamic flow of events with patience, openness, and compassion.

❧

❧ PRACTICE: Taking a Haiku Walk ❧

This practice involves walking mindfully. If you haven't been practicing mindful walking regularly, refer back to chapter 8 for details. Then, the next time you have the opportunity to go outside for a walk, or even if you're just walking out to your car after work or walking through the grocery store, bring your haiku awareness with you. You're likely to begin seeing familiar things for the first time, or to see them in entirely new ways. As I walked out to the mailbox one evening, I approached this rote daily task with haiku awareness and noticed that my neighborhood is a much richer environment than I consider it to be, full of sounds and sensations:

> Sound of feet
> The wet evening pavement
> Cool autumn drizzle

Begin by simply walking mindfully, and stay with this for several minutes. Then open all of your senses with haiku awareness, constructing your haiku as you continue your mindful walk. If you're at a loss, simply direct each line at a specific sense, as in the sight, tactile sensation, and smell construct outlined in the previous practice. When you return from your walk, you can write your new haiku here:

Did you notice things that have always been there for the first time or with new awareness? If so, what were they and what did you notice about them?

Did awakening your senses transform your experience of walking in any way? How did your haiku walk compare to walking as you usually do?

Through this practice, you can see how every experience you have presents an opportunity to connect with your haiku awareness. Pausing and attending to your sensory awareness will often reduce any fear-based reactions to whatever is occurring, allowing you to experience the moment spaciously and embrace your intimate interrelationship with everything around you. Remember, your life goes on with or without you. Haiku awareness is a way to show up and embrace the wonder, simplicity, and joy of your life as it unfolds.

SUMMARY

Haiku awareness builds on the practices you learned in chapter 8, helping you suffuse all of the activities of your daily life with more awareness and mindfulness. The beauty of haiku awareness is that you can take it anywhere. As with focusing on your breath, nothing special is required beyond pausing to connect with whatever is occurring. It's another way of finding your pause and letting go of habitual ways of living. As you may have noticed, living on autopilot isn't confined to basic activities like eating, walking, and driving. In fact, some of the most acute suffering we experience comes from approaching relationships in this way. Think of how liberating it could be to relate to others with this same mindfulness, taking a moment to pause before responding, and considering that each interaction holds the potential for a new beginning.

CHAPTER 10

Spacious Relationships

By now, you're familiar with how fear activates big deal mind, which utilizes a variety of tactics to protect the solid self—an illusory identity felt as fixed and unchanging. Big deal mind also has a tendency to experience others as fixed and unchanging solid selves. This leads to a great deal of suffering as we respond to ourselves and others based on preconceived notions that often aren't relevant or useful to the situation at hand.

Of course, each of us is much more fluid, changing in both subtle and major ways in response to life events. When we let go of the solid self, we become more capable of responding from a place of patience, openness, and compassion. You've explored this process in a variety of practices that relate to your everyday activities, as well as your perception of yourself and the world around you. In this chapter, we'll shift the focus and start to bring spaciousness to the world of relationships so that you can begin to relate to others as they are, not as you believe them to be. This is an excellent foundation for building spacious, mindful, and responsive relationships. You can use this approach with anyone—your partner, your children, a clerk in a store, or the driver in front of you—to build relationships that are more genuine and compassionate. Given how much potential this has to enhance your quality of life and well-being, this may well be the most important chapter in the book. Take time to really embrace and work with the practices in this chapter, and have patience and compassion for yourself as you learn this new way of relating to others.

SOLID SELF AND THE ME VS. YOU DUALITY

Suffering and conflicts in relationships arise when you create distinctions between yourself, your experiences, and others in your life, leading to an experience of duality—a you that is separate from the other person. This sense of duality reinforces a perception of the other person as a possible threat. Big deal mind can keep you focused on this perceived threat in an ongoing series of fear-based reactions that only strengthen the veils of illusion, delusion, attachment, and aggression. Unfortunately, it's all too likely that your reactions will elicit fear-based reactions from the other person, so the ongoing cycle of mindless reaction, misunderstanding, and conflict continues.

When fear controls your relationships, it's as if you're a ball in a pinball machine, bouncing from one interaction to another. With no sense of balance or compassion, you bounce off not only others and their fear-based reactions, but also memories from your past and anticipation of the future. Take a moment to reflect on this: Do you ever notice that when you're in a bad mood, others seem to be in a bad mood, too, or that when your mood is low, others seem more irritating? I once heard a wonderful Zen saying that speaks to this: "You are none other than me with another face and another name." So the next time you become reactive and judgmental toward others or their thoughts, feelings, and behaviors, ask yourself, is there anything about this person that reminds me of myself?

⁓ PRACTICE: Looking at How You Create Duality ⁓

This practice will help you get a firsthand look at the mind's propensity for creating duality in relationships. It will help you notice how your opinions and judgments transform others into a solid self, and how you use your distinctions to justify perceiving the other as a potential threat.

First you'll spend some time mindfully meditating on a specific person and your relationship with that person, then you'll record the distinctions you see between yourself and that person. Don't worry if some of the things you write aren't very flattering to you or the other person. In fact, that's an important part of the process: recognizing and acknowledging the ways these distinctions create rifts, judgments, and misunderstandings. For example, one woman resisted putting down her husband's weight as a distinction. She thought this judgment wasn't very nice of her. However, by acknowledging that she saw him this way, she was able to recognize that attachment to this judgment was an ongoing cause of her aggressive reactions to him.

Adopt the attitude of mindfulness and spend a few moments doing center point breathing, reconnecting with the pause at the end of each out breath.

Bring to mind an important relationship. It can be someone you get along with or someone with whom you have conflict. Take a few minutes to simply be in the presence of that person in your mind and heart.

Next, take some time to fill in the table below, writing down all of the ways you see that other person as different from you. Be honest here.

Finally, take some time to contemplate and answer the questions that follow the table.

Personality	Tone of voice and communication style	Behaviors	Appearance

Why do you think it's important for big deal mind to remain attached to your distinctions?

_____

_____

_____

_____

How do your judgments and distinctions result in conflict in this relationship?

_____

_____

_____

Take a moment to reflect on what feared loss your distinctions might be protecting against. What attachments do those distinctions reflect?

_____

_____

_____

_____

Once you've identified what you're attached to, consider whether what you're holding on to, whether thoughts, beliefs, material objects, or other people, really brings you lasting happiness. If it does, how so? And if it doesn't, how so?

_____

_____

_____

_____

Again, that Zen saying is very helpful here: "You are none other than me with a different name and a different face." In the face of distinctions, use this insight to remind yourself to go easy on them and yourself. This will allow you to simply watch what's occurring, including your fears and distinctions, without trying to figure things out, analyze, or judge what's occurring. As you develop your capacity to watch with patience, openness, and compassion, you'll become more able to embrace yourself and the other person at the same time.

PROTECTIVE STRATEGIES

Relationships are often influenced by the fear that some part of you isn't acceptable to another. As a result, you may resort to fear-based reactions in an attempt to protect that aspect of yourself from injury or exposure. Another possibility is that you may reject that part of yourself, or yourself as a whole.

For example, if you're a parent, the way your children navigate through life can be interpreted as a challenge to your sense of worth as a parent. Seeing your children making questionable choices in how they handle their money, their relationships, drugs and alcohol, their education, and the people they associate with can all affect how you end up feeling about yourself as a parent. If their choices aren't healthy, productive, or what you think they should be, you may feel flawed or deficient as a parent. Because this feeling is painful and unacceptable, you may begin to reject it and employ various tactics to minimize it. From this protective, reactive stance, you perceive your child as a threat to your sense of self and fear being exposed as a failure. Rather than acknowledge or expose that fear, you may end up blaming, criticizing, rejecting, or trying to control your child. But when fear reduces your ability to respond with a spacious sense of patience, openness, and compassion, you're actually creating a greater disconnection between yourself and your child, and between yourself and your value of being a good parent.

To cover deep feelings of fear in relationships, big deal mind often uses three protective strategies: hiding out, lashing out, and tuning out. Throughout life, we're frequently bombarded with messages about how we don't measure up, aren't good enough, or aren't doing something right. When we internalize these messages, we can get stuck in a fear-based reaction mode as we anticipate making yet another mistake, having to take another criticism, or the next thing that will go wrong.

Carrying a chronic sense that something is wrong with you sets up resistance to what is. This entraps you in a cycle of mindless reactivity and protective strategies. These strategies often show up in the form of judgments, jealousy, pride, or a sense of superiority. While these behaviors can be effective at protecting your solid self, they also erect walls around your tenderness, vulnerability, and loving-kindness. When your heart is confined and shut off in this way, you're likely to experience others as a threat or, at best, as a nuisance or interfering. As always with mindfulness, the first key to transformation is awareness. To that end, let's take a more in-depth look at hiding out, lashing out, and tuning out so that you can begin to identify when you're using these protective strategies.

Hiding Out

Hiding out is a type of running away, the *flight* part of the fight, flight, or freeze reaction to a perceived threat. You may hide out when you feel fearful and don't want to acknowledge it or don't want others to see your fear. Hiding out allows you to disconnect not only from others, but also from yourself. You hide out when you don't want to look at or experience your feelings, your behaviors, or how your life is going in general. This also serves to keep others from seeing your true self. There are many ways of disowning yourself or keeping yourself invisible to others. Here are a few common methods, with an example of each. With all of these strategies, the end result is that you don't think, feel, or act in ways that reflect your true nature:

- *Denying:* "I am not controlling."

- *Minimizing:* "My drinking isn't that bad."

- *Rationalizing:* "It wasn't my fault. You would do the same thing if you were in my shoes."

- *Projecting:* "You are a controlling person."

- *Repressing:* "I did not refer to my son as my husband! Why would you say something like that?"

Lashing Out

Lashing out is a manifestation of the *fight* part of the fight, flight, or freeze reaction. You may lash out at others if you don't want them to get close enough to see your fear. You redirect the focus away from you by putting the other person on the defensive so that you don't have to assume responsibility for your thoughts, feelings, or actions. People become afraid of you and are unlikely to see your softer self. Your lashing out keeps others focused on how their behavior "caused" your reaction. All of this serves to deepen the gulf or conflict in relationships. Here are some common methods of lashing out:

- Yelling

- Threatening

- Faultfinding and criticizing

- Being physically aggressive

- Blaming

- Being suspicious

- Demanding reasons or explanations

Tuning Out

Tuning out reflects the *freeze* part of the fight, flight, or freeze reaction. It's a type of numbing that prevents anyone and anything from getting to your soft or tender spots. It's a way of maintaining an uninvolvement in your life. You tune out when you no longer want to be in relationship with yourself, your life, or others in your life. Depression is a common way of tuning out. The very nature of depression is to deaden yourself on many different levels at the same time. The end result is loneliness. Here are some other common ways of tuning out, along with an example of each:

- *Distracting:* If your partner is trying to discuss potential overspending, you might say, "Did you remember to call the plumber?"

- *Ignoring:* If your partner or a friend asks how your day was, you might keep reading the paper without responding.

- *Forgetting:* Failing to remember important events or responsibilities, such as anniversaries, birthdays, meetings, or picking up kids at school, is a common form of tuning out in relationships.

- *Attending to external distractions:* In the midst of a difficult conversation, you might say, "Did someone just pull into our driveway?

153

Marcus's Story

Marcus, age nineteen, came to see me at his parents' insistence. He was living at home and going to college, where he had just completed his freshman year. He was pursuing a degree in either art or graphic design. In high school, he had received local, state, and national awards for his art and design work, but in his first year at college his grades were slipping, and his parents were disappointed. He was considering not going back to school the next year. He'd also recently lost his job because of calling in sick too often, which his parents suspected was actually due to hangovers. They were clearly frustrated about Marcus's lack of responsibility.

Marcus felt his parents were making a big deal out of everything, and he was tired of always fighting with them. When asked what his plans were, he was unclear about what he wanted and what goals he was pursuing. He just knew it was something with art.

In my first few sessions with Marcus, he spent much of his time and focus on how he felt his parents were behaving toward him. "They want me to be like my older sister. She always got good grades, and now she's working at my dad's accounting firm. All I hear is about how great she is. I can't live up to their expectations. They even get on me about cleaning up my room. I feel like I'm still in middle school! Sure, I go out and party a lot; it's the only way I get any relief from the pressure to be what they want me to be. They just don't understand, and their nagging isn't helping."

I talked with Marcus about how conflicts are often driven by fear and helped him identify some of the protective strategies he was using with his parents. At the following session, I asked him to identify the protective strategies his parents were using, and at the end of that session I asked him to bring a sketch pad and some colored pencils to work with next time.

The next week I adapted the theater practice so that a blank sheet on his sketch pad would serve as the screen. I asked him to see his parents when they were upset with him and then draw what they looked like to him when they were "on his case."

When he finished. he looked at the images and said, "Wow, a lot of energy there." When I asked what the energy was, he said, "Fear. Man, my parents are really freaked out by all this. I think I see it now. When they get scared, I get scared, and then we fight. Every time I argue back, they get more scared—and so do I! It becomes a mutual freak-out fest!"

During subsequent sessions, Marcus commented that since that session, every time he and his parents had some conflict all he could see were the drawings he'd done. He also said, "I'm not arguing back as much. Now I can see how that just makes all the fear worse." Then he told me about a discussion he'd had with his dad, saying, "I found myself able to really listen to him." He'd asked his dad, "Are you afraid that I'm going to be a failure?" In response, his dad sighed and said that this was his biggest fear. Marcus was able to tell his dad that he didn't want to be a failure, either, but that right now he just didn't know exactly what to do and which direction to go. His dad shared that he had faced a similar dilemma, because his father had wanted him to go into medicine, but he choose finance instead.

Marcus said, "I realized that my dad and I really aren't that different. I could finally see that he wants the same thing I do. Neither one of us wants me to fail. Now we can actually talk about it without too much conflict. I still think he's pretty hard on me, but at least I can see that it's about his fear and not so much about what he thinks of me. What a relief!"

❧ PRACTICE: Responding, Rather Than Reacting, to Conflict ❧

This practice will help you begin to explore spaciousness in the midst of conflict. You can do this either in your imagination or in real life. Because bringing patience, openness, and compassion to conflict is unfamiliar and may feel counterintuitive or just plain wrong, it's best to practice through visualization first, then move to real-life situations, which is how this practice is set up. When practicing in real-life situations, start with situations that aren't highly charged and with people who are generally supportive. In fact, there's no way to ensure that the other person will unknowingly participate in a conflict, so you may need to wait for conflict situations to arise before you can practice in real life. This approach incorporates the practice of watching, naming, and letting go of thoughts, emotions, and sensations, as you learned in chapter 2, so you may want to go back and review that practice before continuing.

Assume the attitude of mindfulness, then take some time to settle into center point breathing and connect with the pause at the end of your out breath. As you rest in your pause, remember that with any practice of mindfulness, it's crucial to start with extending patience and kindness toward yourself. No one is perfect, including in mindfulness. So embrace yourself, struggles and all, with patience, openness, and compassion. If you don't start here, it will be difficult to genuinely extend this attitude toward others.

Imagine yourself in the presence of someone you have a conflict with. Bring the conflict to mind and really envision the details of your interaction: what each of you might say, tone of voice and body language for both of you, and even details in the environment around you.

As you do this, remain connected to your pause and bring gentle awareness to your fearful reactions. As you begin to tune in to these reactions, simply name them as they occur, being sure to note thoughts, feelings, and sensations—everything from wanting to interrupt, needing to be right, or thinking of your response to breaking eye contact, shortness of breath, or a tight jaw. Just name them and let them go, all the while remaining connected with your pause. Do this for several minutes, or longer if you like, then take some time to contemplate and answer the following questions.

What did you notice as you remained connected with your pause and placed your awareness on your fear-based reactions and naming them?

_____

_____

_____

_____

What reactions did you notice and name? Were they physical? Were they particular protective strategies? Which ones?

_____

_____

_____

_____

Did you notice a shift in the way you were thinking or feeling? What sort of changes occurred, and how did that feel?

_____

_____

_____

_____

Did you notice any changes in your thoughts and feelings about the other person?

_____

_____

_____

_____

The next time you have an interaction with this person, go through this entire practice once again.

First connect with your breath and your pause and extend patience and compassion toward yourself. Then, as the interaction plays out, bring gentle awareness to your fearful reactions, naming all of the thoughts, feelings, and sensations that arise as you interact, then letting them go. Pay particular attention to how this approach helps you manage your reactions and avoid falling back on habitual protective strategies. Then take some time to contemplate and answer the following questions.

What did you notice as you remained connected with your pause and placed your awareness on your fear-based reactions and naming them?

_____

_____

_____

_____

_____

What reactions did you notice and name? Were they physical? Were they particular protective strategies? Which ones?

_____

_____

_____

_____

_____

Did you notice a shift in the way you were thinking or feeling? What sort of changes occurred, and how did that feel?

_____

_____

_____

_____

_____

Did you notice any changes in your thoughts and feelings about the other person?

_____

_____

_____

_____

_____

Whenever you find yourself in a conflict situation, remember to return to your pause, then notice, name, and let go of your reactions before you respond. This will help you move a bit beyond your edge of reluctance and fear and gain more experience in living and relating from a place of mindful presence. As you begin to respond rather than react, you'll notice that your relationships will take on a greater depth and that other people are more likely to respond rather than react, as well.

Keeping a relationship journal would be of great benefit here. As you continue to practice this approach in your relationships, take the time to write about your experiences. You might record your protective strategies, describe how you're working with the fear that drives these strategies, and then write about how connecting with your pause, then naming and letting go helps you become more mindfully responsive. This is a powerful way to track your progress and see how you're becoming more willing to soften your protective armor and open to the flow of the actual experiences in your relationships. It will also help you see where you're still closing down; these are excellent opportunities to apply the approach in this practice.

PATIENCE, OPENNESS, AND COMPASSION IN RELATIONSHIPS

Up to this point in the chapter, you've spent some time learning how big deal mind reacts to perceived threats, the strategies you typically use in these situations, and what your fear may be about. You've learned to notice these reactions and resist the urge to fall back on habitual protective behaviors. You may have noticed that when you give these reactions plenty of space, they often recede on their own. Within that space, you'll find that you can respond and relate with patience, openness, and compassion. This invites the other person to feel safe and understood in your presence and is the key to practicing spacious presence in your relationships. Let's take yet another look at these key qualities, this time from the perspective of relationships.

Patience

In the introduction I described patience as allowing any given situation to evolve without imposing a need to manipulate, influence, and or control the outcome. It means simply being with whatever is occurring, without fear-based, self-protective reactions. Practicing patience in your relationships is an invitation to wait for a mindful response to arise as you allow the flow of your experience to fully evolve without interrupting or distracting. Once your experience becomes fully manifest, mindful responses often arise naturally.

When you invite patience into your relationships, you rest in the flow of whatever is occurring. You recognize how your relationships are a reflection of the ever-unfolding flow inherent in life, as you and those around you are in a constant state of change. Even when those changes are subtle, don't be lulled into believing that they're insignificant.

When you practice patience, you're simply in the presence of others, life, and yourself, allowing whatever is emerging through the relationship to develop fully. Affirming your willingness to stay present and patient with whatever is occurring is a powerful way to communicate that what the person is thinking, feeling, and expressing is important. Patience doesn't imply agreeing or trying to fix anything; it simply expresses that you're willing to stand by and stand with the other person even in the face of difficulties. It erases the "me versus you" duality and creates a "we."

As you practice remaining connected with loving-kindness (toward others and yourself), you invite an open dialogue based on mutual respect. As your attachment to solid self dissipates into the spaciousness created by patience, your mode of responding will shift away from reactiveness. Rather than wondering how you can protect yourself, you'll consider how you can support others. Patience can be like a container in which you hold the suffering of others, helping them feel less alone.

∿ PRACTICE: Cultivating Patience ∿

During the next three practices, identify one person in your life with whom you have a significant relationship. Then for one week, work on staying patient with the flow of what is occurring in your relationship with this person. Strive to avoid resorting to Big Deal Mind's protective strategies. Watch with clear seeing, the ways you habitually resort to trying to impose, control, manipulate, or otherwise influence the outcome of the interaction. Allow the relationship to evolve fully. Record how you found yourself responding when practicing mindful patience.

160

_____

_____

_____

_____

_____

This practice of patience will also help you understand the universal nature of suffering. Many of us have a tendency to shrink from suffering in all of its forms. As you come to understand it as part of the human condition, you'll be able to simply be with it and begin to see it as something that creates a bond between you and all of your fellow human beings. This allows you to remain connected to others regardless of their circumstances, which invites others to acknowledge and share their suffering. Ultimately, being open to and sharing our suffering diminishes the amount of distress associated with it.

❧

Openness

Openness in relationships is characterized by willingness to be receptive to other people's thoughts, feelings, actions, and needs. It allows you to drop any resistance or fear-based reactions to the dynamic flow of the relationship as it unfolds. With openness, you can explore what each experience offers you. When you don't resort to fear-based protective strategies, you're able to be genuinely present. You'll be interested in learning about the other person, and this will be evident, creating more trust and honesty in the relationship. This invites the other person to express openly and from a place of tenderness and kindness.

Developing more of a sense of curiosity about others is an important way of creating openness in relationships. Curiosity keeps the focus off you and your big deal mind and on others and their experience. Rather than seeing others as solid selves, with unchanging and predictable personalities, let yourself remain curious, approaching them with a curiosity that asks, "So, who are you today?"

If you're like most people, when in conversation you may spend a fair amount of time thinking about what you'll say next. Instead, take the time to really listen to the other person, and be sure to ask about anything you don't fully understand. Then express your appreciation for what the other person has shared. With curiosity, you can remain open to others, even amidst their struggles and fear-based reactions.

❧ PRACTICE: Cultivating Openness ❧

For one week, work on remaining curious in your interactions with this person. Watch with clear seeing how big deal mind attempts to disconnect you from the other person by employing judgments, opinions, and criticisms. Strive to keep a sense of fresh perspective on what is occurring. Even if the content is "old news," stay open to what is indeed occurring. Record how you found yourself responding when practicing mindful openness.

_____

_____

_____

_____

_____

The key is remembering that it isn't about you. When you're open and spaciously present with others, you understand that what others are communicating is important and meaningful to them. It doesn't matter if it's important to you; you appreciate the communication because it conveys what's important to the other person. In fact, this is where the seeds of compassion lie. When you remain patient and open to whatever others wish to communicate, you begin to understand how their experience feels from their perspective.

Compassion

Compassion is frequently defined as being in the presence another person's suffering with the desire to alleviate that suffering. This requires intention and commitment, as you must be willing to let the other person's suffering touch your own. It also requires mindfulness of your internal state. You're likely to find that this sort of deep connection can elicit fear-based reactions. Acknowledge this when it occurs and resist the urge to act from a place of fear, then return to simply being with the other person.

Compassion isn't an intellectual experience; it's a direct experience of the universal nature of suffering. As such, it requires your willingness and courage to let the other person's suffering touch your own without resorting to protective strategies. Your simply maintaining spacious presence for the other person's experience, without trying to fix the situation, allows them to feel "felt" and facilitates true healing. Rather than rushing toward a solution, take the time to acknowledge and be with the other person's suffering. Approach the person from a place of genuinely wanting to help with their life journey—not helping as in trying to fix things, make things better, or eliminate the problem, but in terms of wanting to fully embrace their experience and how and why it's important to them. Most people communicate because they want to be understood and supported, not be told what to do, much less criticized or dismissed.

An important aspect of inviting compassion into your mindful responses with others is recognizing that other people's feelings and actions arise from their own suffering and from their attachments. You might mistake their behaviors, attitudes, or feelings as stemming from something *you* did or said. If you take the situation personally this way, you begin to create a "me versus you" duality and may feel compelled to resort to habitual protection strategies. When this happens, remember once again that it probably isn't about you. Listen more deeply and feel into the other person's pain to better understand its source. At the same time, maintain a mindful awareness of your own internal state. When you feel compelled to react rather than respond, acknowledge and name those reactions: "Anger. Wanting to be right. Fear. Reaction, reaction, reaction, look at all of those reactions. Urge to interrupt. Thinking of what I'm going to say next."

✍ PRACTICE: Cultivating Compassion ✍

For one week, work on keeping your heart open in your interactions with this person. Understand that the other person's thoughts, feelings, and actions may be coming from a place of their suffering and struggle. Watch with clear seeing how big deal mind attempts to disconnect you by judging the other person. Maintain a compassionate connection with the other person and embrace how their struggles are showing up in any interaction. Record how you found yourself responding when practicing mindful compassion.

_____

_____

_____

_____

Embrace what you have in common with the people you relate to—everyone from those closest to you to those you encounter briefly as you go about your day. This will deepen your feelings of warmth and caring toward others. As others feel your spacious support and empathy, they'll experience the relationship as safe and nonthreatening. One of the most powerful aspects of relating from a place of empathy is learning to trust that an appropriate, compassionate response will arise. You cannot force or construct these responses; you must allow them to emerge.

Tim's Story

Tim, a forty-five-year-old man, had recently lost his wife and teenage daughter in an automobile accident. As he shared his feelings with me, his anguish was terribly deep and his suffering beyond measure. This spoke to my own experiences of loss, and part of me, afraid to feel my own feelings in response, was fast at work distracting me from the pain in the room and trying to find the right "therapeutic" answer to help this man with his pain—and thereby prevent me from contacting my own feelings of loss.

Noticing this, I practiced center point breathing for a few breaths and returned to my pause. Then I found I could sit with him and allow my past loss experiences to facilitate deep empathy for him. When he finished telling his story, he sighed and said, "So what do I do now?"

I rested in my pause, and the response that emerged was "I don't know. Your pain now is too deep for answers."

"Thank you!" he said. "You are the first person who's admitted that they don't know what to say or do. People say such dumb things to try to make me feel better. I think you get it—because I have no idea what to do either."

I said, "This is just one of those times when there's nothing to say or do but just sit with it. Some of our experiences are so deep that they're beyond words or actions. If you want to talk more from your pain, feel free. Sometimes just letting the pain be and not trying to fix it is okay." Then I taught him the center point breathing technique so he could gain access to his pause.

As he also rested in his pause, he was able to gain a perspective that, amidst his pain, he could also feel calm, which helped him feel the possibility of moving through his pain. "In my pause I get glimpses, moments where I'm not consumed by this pain. I will get through this."

Expressing compassion isn't always about doing something to fix the other person's situation, and it isn't about pity or feeling sorry for the person. It's about respecting others' experience enough to allow them to have it on their terms, in their way, but with your support and within a relationship imbued with trust, openness, and safety. Operating as "we," rather than "me helping you," keeps both people connected to the greater flow of the relationship.

GUIDELINES FOR MINDFUL INTERACTIONS

Effectively creating spacious presence in your relationships means approaching others as you've learned to mindfully approach other activities in your life, such as eating, walking, and driving. Simply connecting with your pause and being with the other person with patience, openness, and compassion can go a long way toward fostering connection and trust. However, relationships and communication can be complicated, and sometimes highly charged. Here are some guidelines that will help you optimize your success in approaching important interactions mindfully.

Create the right space for the communication. Choose or create a space that invites a mutual feeling of safety, keeping in mind the needs of both people.

- **Physical space.** Physical proximity communicates interest, so sit close together. But as discussed above, do make sure the space between you is comfortable for both of you.

- **Emotional space.** Check in with yourself and your intentions. Are you approaching this wanting to win, be right, or criticize the other? Creating supportive emotional space means approaching the interaction with patience, openness, and compassion. Take a moment to connect with your pause.

- **Tactile space.** Touch can be misinterpreted, so clarify how touch can be appropriately used in this particular relationship or interaction. For some people, touch may communicate a deep feeling of connection, whereas for others it can be a threatening intrusion. If touching is appropriate and acceptable, use it. It's powerful.

- **Sound space.** Make sure there are minimal auditory intrusions, and also protect the privacy of your interaction by making sure others can't listen in.

- **Smell space.** The sense of smell is the only sense that's directly connected to the amygdala (the part of your memory that stores emotional memories). Smell is a powerful emotional stimulus. For example, if you need to have an important discussion with your partner or child and you've just come home and may be carrying odors from work, take a shower and put on clean clothes so that work odors and body odors won't be a distraction.

- **Uncluttered space.** It's important to eliminate all distractions—outer and inner. This means turning off the stereo or television, moving away from the computer, and putting down newspapers, books, or magazines. Also, make sure you're in a receptive mode. If you feel agitated or upset, ask for some time to center yourself in a place of patience, openness, and compassion. This would be a good time to practice center point breathing. If someone wants to talk and you're in the middle of something, ask to be allowed to finish. Give the person a time frame for when you can talk.

Attend to body language, tone, and communication style. Although verbal communication and choosing one's words carefully are important, we also convey a great deal through body language, tone of voice, and speaking style. In fact, these nonverbal modes of expression can have the effect of undermining or subverting the verbal communication. I'm sure you've had the experience of someone saying one thing to you but communicating something entirely different with body language or tone. This definitely erodes trust, connection, and compassion, so attend to your nonverbal communication closely.

- **Face-to-face position.** As with proximity, a face-to-face position conveys interest, as well as trust. A powerful way to ensure you remain in a face-to-face position is to establish and maintain good eye contact. When you break eye contact, often you've withdrawn into your inner dialogue and broken your connection with the other person. Simply recognize that this has happened, then reconnect.

- **Soften the expression on your face and uncross your legs and arms.** Your body language tends to override whatever you're saying verbally. It's likely that it communicates the true nature of your feelings about the other person. It may also convey whether you feel threatened and have turned to protective strategies.

- **Choose your tone of voice.** Tone of voice, like facial expression and body language, communicates far more than words do. Make sure your tone expresses your intention to remain patient, open, and compassionate. Let the tone resonate from your heart. (Below, you'll find a practice to help you develop this tone.)

- **Wait a moment before you begin to talk.** A helpful way to do this is to assume an attitude of mindfulness and connect with your pause. Take this time to check in with your body language and tone of voice before you respond. Ask yourself, "Am I responding or reacting?" Choose words that reflect your intention to create connection. Are your words communicating "I want to understand" or "You're wrong and I'm determined to prove it to you."

Remain focused on the topic at hand. Big deal mind wants to keep the communication in a "me versus you," fear-based mode and may try to do so by overloading the discussion with numerous topics. This almost guarantees that you won't find closure or resolution on most issues. Keep the discussion to one topic at a time. Also, resolve each topic before moving on, making sure both of you agree that the topic has been reasonably resolved.

Give acknowledgments. Be sure to include simple phrases that communicate your genuine interest throughout the conversation, such as "I understand why this is important to you," "I appreciate your point of view," and "That must be frustrating [sad, annoying, and so on] for you." These shouldn't be stock phrases delivered by rote; they should genuinely express to the other person that you want to deepen the understanding and closeness between you. Acknowledgment can also be nonverbal, in the form of nodding, smiling, or touching if appropriate.

Choose compassionate responses. Mindful responses create and maintain a sense of "we," rather than "me versus you." When you approach conflicts, disagreements, and difficult emotions with a greater sense of patience, openness, and compassion, you're less likely to view them as threats emanating from the other person. As discussed above, you can use nonverbal communication to convey your compassionate response to the other. It's also important to use words that will encourage the other person to draw closer to you. For example, rather than offering a reactive statement like "You're wrong," you can remain in the presence of the disagreement and offer a spacious response, such as "I understand why you feel the way you do, and I think we can find a way to solve this situation." Use words that invite a genuine feeling of spacious permission for each of you to think, feel, and act as you are. Here are some words and phrases that will emphasize your connection:

- Yes.

- We…

- I understand.

- I appreciate why you think [or feel] the way you do.

- How can I help?

- You have every right to how you feel.

- Let me think about that.

- Tell me more about that.

- I'd be happy to.

- Is this what you mean?

❧ PRACTICE: Creating the Heart Tone in Your Voice ❧

Tone of voice is a lot like personal space. What feels natural and neutral to one person may sound like yelling to another. When people perceive a tone of voice to be threatening, it's natural to react with protective strategies. As a result, the connection is lost and the conversation is derailed. Another possibility is that tone of voice becomes the focus of the discussion, again derailing the conversation.

Here's a tip that will reduce this cause of misunderstanding. Most of us typically talk from the throat region. If the interaction involves any degree of stress, this region will tighten up, forcing you to push your voice harder in order to get through the constriction. The tone and volume of your voice will change in ways that others may perceive as increasingly aggressive. In this practice, you'll explore how to create a tone of voice that generates a sense of warmth in both yourself and the other. I call it the heart tone. Basically, it involves speaking from your heart region.

> *Put one hand over your throat and talk as you normally do.*
>
> *Feel the vibration that your words create in this region.*
>
> *Keeping your hand on your throat region, put your other hand over your heart. As you continue to speak normally (probably from your throat region), note the sensations in the hand over your throat and how they differ from the sensations in the hand over your heart.*
>
> *Adjust the volume and tone of your voice until the hand over your heart begins to feel your voice coming from your heart region. As you move your voice energy from your throat to your heart, pay attention to what this is like.*
>
> *Move your voice back to your throat region and note any differences.*

Take some time continue to explore the heart tone, then use the space below to describe any differences you note—not just differences in the sensation in each hand, but also in how you feel overall when you speak from your heart region, rather than from your throat.

_____

_____

_____

_____

Spend some time practicing the heart tone on your own. Once it feels a bit familiar, begin to use it as often as you like. It's especially helpful when you're engaged in a difficult conversation. Try it and see how it affects the interaction. Over time, you'll find that it's much easier to be aware of when your voice begins to constrict and get trapped in the throat region. This shift is likely to be associated with a return to a protective stance. It may signal that you're disconnecting from your own heart, and therefore the other person's heart, and moving back toward your head and big deal mind. When you can mindfully return to speaking from the heart, you'll be more open and connected to the other, enabling you to make the most of the precious opportunity to enrich your life through the relationship. Likewise, if others complain about your tone of voice, try switching to the heart tone.

SUMMARY

Creating mindfulness in relationships can be challenging. Recognizing your fear-based reactions and resisting the urge to engage in habitual, ingrained protective strategies is hard work and may take some time. And no matter how successful you are in this, there are no guarantees that the other person will respond in kind. But if you show up mindfully, with patience, openness, and compassion, you'll create an atmosphere of connection and trust that emphasizes commonalities rather than distinctions, and that bridges the "me versus you" divide, inviting the other person to join with you as a "we." In the next chapter, we'll look at how to expand this approach even further. Using the ancient practice of loving-kindness meditation, you'll extend compassion in ever-widening circles, starting with yourself and extending outward, ultimately to all beings, the planet, and the entire universe.

CHAPTER 11

First from the Heart

All too often, we operate from a place of hurt, focusing on perceived injustices and how we've been wronged. The resulting fear-based reactions serve to deepen the distinctions and disconnections between us, fracturing friendships, marriages, and work relationships and leading to discord between nations, factions, races, and religions. Imagine what a different place the world could be if we instead focused on operating from the heart, extending love and compassion to everyone—even strangers, difficult people, and perceived enemies—and ultimately to all beings. This approach is actually an ancient practice, known as loving-kindness meditation, that's as relevant today as when it originated over 2,500 years ago. In loving-kindness meditation, you extend well-wishes and goodwill from your heart to the hearts of others, cultivating what I call heart presence. From this place, you experience and express your deep connection with others, and those you relate to will feel it.

THE HEART: MORE THAN JUST A PUMP

For centuries, numerous mindfulness practices have emphasized the role of the heart in bringing forth feelings of love, patience, and compassion. The heart has also long been seen as the center for experiences of love, awe, inspiration, art, and music, and our connection with the Divine. In the modern, Western world, this view of the heart has often been dismissed as mystical, metaphysical, or whimsical. Fortunately, our understanding of the heart is changing. Science is catching up and recognizing what mystics, artists, healers, and philosophers have long known: The heart really *is* the seat of our emotions.

We now know that the heart is more than just a mechanical pump. A new branch of scientific and medical inquiry called *neurocardiology* is demonstrating that the heart isn't just a pump; it's a sensory organ with a nervous system extensive enough to qualify it as a "heart-brain" (Amour and Ardell 1994). The heart's nervous system contains around forty thousand neurons, making it astoundingly capable of communicating with cells, nerves, and organs throughout the body. Neurocardiology is also examining how the rhythm of the heart influences the nervous system, immune system, endocrine system, emotions, intelligence, and cognitive function. Communication between the heart and the brain is a two-way street, with each influencing the other.

Directing positive, loving feelings toward your heart region creates a measurable and positive influence throughout all of the networks of the body (McCraty 2003). In fact, when you direct loving feelings to your heart region, your brain waves become more coherent, generating a deep sense of calm and well-being. A study conducted at the HeartMath Research Center (Rein, Atkinson, and McCraty 1995) demonstrated that focusing loving attention to the heart region led to reductions in stress levels, which in turn helped boost immunity, reduce tension, and improve mental clarity.

THE PAUSE AND LOVING-KINDNESS

The practices in this chapter combine center point breathing with the ancient practice of loving-kindness meditation, which was first taught by the Buddha and is also known as *metta meditation*. The Sanskrit word *metta* has many translations, including loving-kindness, benevolence, goodwill, friendliness, love, sympathy, and interest in others. Over the centuries the practice has evolved, and perhaps in response to the troubled times we live in, current interest in loving-kindness meditation has led to a proliferation of forms. This chapter explores applying heart mindfulness by way of metta meditation as first taught by the Buddha. In this meditation, you'll direct spacious, loving, compassionate feelings first toward yourself and then toward others in increasingly wider circles, eventually encompassing all living beings and the entire universe, and finally directing that energy back to yourself once again.

This is a powerful practice for cultivating heart presence and can generate profound emotions. Too often, daily life experiences shut off our connection with our heart, and thus our true emotional life. The intention of loving-kindness practice is to help you create spaciousness around your heart and reconnect to your core—your loving, patient, and compassionate self.

~ PRACTICE: Loving-Kindness Meditation ~

In this meditation, you'll use the pause in center point breathing to extend loving-kindness in a sequence of eight levels:

1. Yourself

2. Loved ones

3. Friends

4. Someone in difficulty

5. Strangers or people you have a passing acquaintance with

6. Difficult people or enemies

7. All living beings

8. Back to yourself

When doing this or any loving-kindness meditation, it's important to connect with your own heart and allow your loving-kindness statements to emanate from your heart region. As you extend outward to others, imagine them sitting in front of you. Say their name and get a feeling for their presence, then offer your phrase of loving-kindness to them. Feel as though you're holding their hearts in your own. Create a true heart-to-heart connection via your loving-kindness statement.

As always in mindfulness meditation, whenever your attention wanders, don't worry about it or judge yourself. Just gently notice that this has occurred and return to your pause and your loving-kindness statements. The entire process will take about ten to fifteen minutes. Be sure to find a quiet, comfortable place to practice, where you won't be disturbed.

Sit in a comfortable upright position, close your eyes, and assume the attitude of mindfulness. Pay attention to the rhythm of your breath, then begin to practice center point breathing. Breathe for several cycles, resting in your pause. As you continue resting in your pause, focus your attention on the region of your heart. Then, throughout this practice, each time you return to your pause make a statement of compassion, as outlined below.

1. *Start with a simple loving and compassionate phrase directed toward yourself, such as "May I live in safety," "May I be happy," "May I be healthy," "May I live peacefully," or "May I be free of suffering." For the purposes of describing this practice, I'll use the phrase "May you be happy," but feel free to substitute any phrase that feels right to you. As you rest in your pause, focus your mindfulness and loving-kindness statement on your heart region, and simply rest there with that experience. Don't rush to the next stage. Take your time and be patient. Be with your pause. Allow feelings of appreciation and gratitude to arise within your own heart. This place will set the tone for the rest of the practice. It's crucial that you genuinely feel loving-kindness in your heart toward yourself before extending it outward.*

2. *Extend your loving-kindness statement toward a loved one. This may be a family member, a partner, someone who has helped you in your life, or someone who inspires you. Become aware of that person's presence, connect with your pause, then direct your phrase of loving-kindness to them: "May my loved one be happy." (Of course, it's fine to use the person's name.) Allow feelings of loving-kindness to emanate from your heart toward your loved one.*

3. *Extend your loving-kindness statement toward a friend, choosing someone you're less intimate with but still have goodwill and affection for. Become aware of that person, connect with your pause, then direct your phrase of loving-kindness toward your friend: "May my friend be happy."*

4. *Extend your loving-kindness statement toward someone you know who's having a difficult time right now. Perhaps this person has experienced a loss, illness, or injury or is going through a difficult time in life. Bring this person to mind, connect with your pause, then direct your phrase of loving-kindness toward the person.*

5. *Extend your loving-kindness statement toward a passing acquaintance or someone you hardly know—maybe a checkout person at the supermarket where you shop, a gas-station attendant, or someone else you see periodically. Bring this person to mind, connect with your pause, then direct your phrase of loving-kindness toward the person.*

6. *Now here's a tough one: Extend your loving-kindness statement to someone you're struggling with who has hurt or angered you. Bring this person to mind and really spend time resting in your pause. It may take a while before you can genuinely extend loving-kindness toward this person, from your heart to the other's heart. When your heart has softened, direct your phrase of loving-kindness to the person. Take a deep breath and return to your pause.*

7. *Widen your sphere and extend your loving-kindness statement to all living beings, human and otherwise. Think of connecting your heart with all of the hearts beating throughout the world. Then widen your sphere to include the planet and the universe as you understand it. Imagine the earth as a heart, beating with life. Connect your loving-kindness to this beating heart, then do the same with the entire universe. Rest here and let yourself feel how your loving-kindness is radiating out from your heart to encompass all life on all levels: all people, all animals, all creatures on the earth, in the air, in the water, all those in existence—near and far, known to you and unknown to you, those being born, those dying.*

8. *Finally, rest in your pause and bring these feelings back to yourself, extending your loving-kindness statement to yourself once again. Rest here and bathe in the beauty of this mindfulness meditation, feeling your heart extending infinitely all around you in a boundless way, leaving no one out in your aspiration that all beings may live in safety, be happy, be healthy, and live with ease. Rest here, radiating loving-kindness outward while at the same time receiving loving-kindness. Allow yourself to experience how the feelings that are emerging come from the immense spaciousness of your pause.*

9. *When you feel ready, open your eyes and see if you can bring this energy with you throughout the day.*

10. *Now take some time to contemplate and answer the following questions, considering both emotions and physical sensations when you respond:*

What did you notice when you directed your compassionate attention toward your heart?

_____

_____

_____

_____

_____

What began to occur as you expanded your compassionate spaciousness to include a loved one?

_____

_____

_____

_____

What began to occur as you expanded your compassionate spaciousness to include a friend?

_____

_____

_____

_____

What began to occur as you expanded your compassionate spaciousness to someone experiencing difficulty?

_____

_____

_____

_____

What began to occur as you expanded your compassionate spaciousness to include a stranger?

_____

_____

_____

_____

_____

What began to occur as you expanded your compassionate spaciousness to a difficult person or an enemy?

_____

_____

_____

_____

_____

What began to occur as you expanded your compassionate spaciousness to embrace all life, in all directions?

_____

_____

_____

_____

_____

What began to occur as you brought your loving-kindness and compassionate spaciousness back to yourself?

_____

_____

_____

_____

What difficulties did you have with this practice? Did you perhaps feel some resistance to extending compassion to certain people or resistance to extending compassionate attention to yourself?

_____

_____

_____

_____

As you continue to work with this practice, make it your own. Feel free to create your own phrases. I've had clients and workshop participants tell me they've incorporated poetry and song lyrics into their practice. Whatever phrases you choose, by extending loving-kindness outward in this fashion you open yourself to connecting in many ways, such as including rather than excluding, accepting rather than rejecting, understanding rather that judging, and caring rather than being indifferent.

Karen's Story

Karen, a forty-seven-year old married woman who is a physician at a local clinic, was suffering a great deal because of being betrayed by her close friend, Ariana, who worked as an administrator at another clinic in a nearby town. Over the years, Karen and Ariana had shared many important and meaningful life experiences: marriage, the births of their children, the deaths of family members, vacations, frustrations with work, and so much more. Ariana had been like a sister to Karen—the sister she never had when she was growing up.

One day Karen was asked to come into the office of the director of the clinic where she worked. When she arrived, he and the head of human resources told her that a serious report of unprofessional practice had been brought against the clinic, citing Karen as the offender. Specifically, she was cited for speaking poorly about a physician in another clinic. Even though she had a stellar performance record, she was severely reprimanded. She was crestfallen, as she'd always prided herself on maintaining a high level of professional conduct and couldn't recall having made the statements she was accused of. In fact, she referred patients to that clinic frequently.

Eventually, Karen learned that Ariana was the person who brought the complaint against her. Apparently, one of Karen's patients wasn't happy with the care Karen provided and sought services at the clinic where Ariana worked. This patient told Ariana that Karen recommended against going to the other clinic because the physicians there weren't very good. But in fact, Karen hadn't said this at all; the entire incident was fabricated by the patient.

Karen was angry and hurt that Ariana didn't bring this concern directly to her so they could work it out—and also that Ariana even believed this patient, a relative stranger, in the first place, rather than having faith in Karen's integrity. Instead, she began distancing herself from her friend. This was painful, since their relationship had been especially meaningful and fulfilling for her, and Karen was grief stricken at losing the relationship. In fact, she felt the pain so acutely that it began affecting her physical health as well. She became increasingly anxious and irritable and felt the need to take medication to help her with this.

Later that year, Karen learned loving-kindness meditation and found it to be very helpful in her healing process. Soon afterward, she found herself in a position where she was going to have to resume contact with this Ariana. She felt a great deal of anxiety as she revisited her emotions regarding this relationship, and people gave her all sorts of advice, mostly along the lines of confronting Ariana about what she had done. But as she continued to work with loving-kindness meditation,

Karen experienced a profound insight. As she put it, "First from the heart, then from the hurt."

This is truly a place of compassionate spaciousness. With the heart presence Karen had developed through loving-kindness meditation, she could see that confronting Ariana from her hurt would threaten Ariana, make her feel unsafe, and put her on the defensive. On the other hand, maintaining heart presence in relationship to Ariana would allow the right time to address the hurt to emerge. As Karen remained connected to her compassion for her friend's pain and suffering, she developed a deep appreciation that Ariana's behavior was about Ariana's own suffering.

A few months later, Ariana came into Karen's office and closed the door. When she sat down, she started crying and telling Karen how much she missed her and their friendship. She confessed to what she had done and apologized for the way she'd handled the situation. As Ariana softened, she could talk openly about her pain, the difficulties she was having at that time in her life, and how they played out in her actions. While Karen says the friendship isn't nearly as close as it had been, she has once again started to enjoy some of what made their relationship so special.

❧ PRACTICE: Working with Fearful Relationships ❧

This practice is a more in-depth exploration of extending loving-kindness to a person with whom you are in conflict. This isn't because it's somehow more important than extending loving-kindness to others, but because it can be most challenging. The real meat of mindfulness practice occurs when you approach the edge of your comfort zone—that place beyond which you aren't willing to go—and embrace those elements in your life that you routinely retreat from. In all of your work with mindfulness, and especially here, it's important to remember that you can only embrace what's uncomfortable, including other people, once you've made friends with yourself. Only then can you respond mindfully to all those around you.

For this practice, you'll visualize a person who causes you pain or suffering, then extend loving-kindness statements toward that person. As you begin this practice, don't choose someone who has caused intense pain, such as a parent who abandoned you, someone who assaulted you, or a partner who recently betrayed you. Start out with a relationship that's only mildly difficult. With time and as you feel comfortable, you can approach more difficult relationships. Whomever you choose, be sure to pace yourself as you work with this practice. If you start to feel too uncomfortable, take a moment to connect with your pause and regroup. If you wish to apply this practice or other mindfulness approaches to more difficult relationships, it would be a good idea to seek out a qualified therapist to help guide and support you in this part of your healing journey.

> *Assume the attitude of mindfulness. Pay attention to the rhythm of your breath, then begin to practice center point breathing. Breathe for several cycles, connecting with your pause and resting here for a few minutes.*
>
> *As you continue resting in your pause, focus your attention on the region of your heart. Start by allowing feelings of appreciation and gratitude toward yourself to arise in your heart, as this will set the tone for the rest of the practice.*
>
> *Because this practice is difficult, be sure to truly connect with your breath, your pause, and your heart so that you'll feel calm, safe, and supported, then bring to mind a relationship that causes you pain and suffering. Visualize the other person and the important aspects of the conflict fully.*
>
> *As you continue to visualize this person and the situation, extend loving-kindness statements toward the person. Let your loving-kindness statements emanate from your heart region and radiate out toward the other person's heart. Continue to extend loving-kindness toward the person for a few minutes.*
>
> *When you feel ready, open your eyes and take some time to contemplate and answer the following questions, considering both emotions and physical sensations when you respond.*

What did you notice when you extended loving-kindness statements toward this difficult person? Did you feel any resistance, reluctance, fear, or anger?

_____

_____

_____

_____

_____

What were you aware of when you let your loving-kindness statements originate from your heart?

_____

_____

_____

_____

What did you notice when you extended your loving-kindness statements directly toward the heart of the person you visualized?

_____

_____

_____

_____

What experience did you have as you kept extending your loving-kindness statements toward this person? Was it positive or negative?

_____

_____

_____

_____

As you continued to extend loving-kindness statements toward the other person, what changes did you notice emotionally and physically?

_____

_____

_____

_____

The next time you have a chance to interact with this individual, keep your loving-kindness statements in mind and use this practice (silently and internally) as you interact. As soon afterward as practical, return to this page and answer the questions again.

_____

_____

_____

_____

What did you notice when you extended loving-kindness statements toward this difficult person? Did you feel any resistance, reluctance, fear, or anger?

_____

_____

_____

_____

What were you aware of when you let your loving-kindness statements originate from your heart?

_____

_____

_____

_____

What did you notice when you extended your loving-kindness statements directly toward the heart of the person you visualized?

_____

_____

_____

_____

What experience did you have as you kept extending your loving-kindness statements toward this person? Was it positive or negative?

_____

_____

_____

_____

As you continued to extend loving-kindness statements toward the other person, what changes did you notice emotionally and physically?

_____

_____

_____

_____

_____

Although this practice may be highly challenging, it also holds the potential for great rewards. Because relationships with difficult people are often a major source of stress, learning to relate to these people differently—even if they remain the same—is highly beneficial.

SUMMARY

Practicing loving-kindness meditation and developing spacious heart presence is a mind-body event, encompassing all aspects of your existence. Through this practice, you'll develop a profound sense of compassion and expand your ability to express mindful responses from your entire being. By extending heart presence to difficult people, you may begin to live with greater ease as you replace conflict and hostility with an intention of loving-kindness. As you extend your heart toward all life, the planet, and the entire universe, you'll feel a profound sense of connection to all of creation and know that you are an essential part of all that is. This is truly a pathway to peace and connection.

Epilogue

As you've worked your way through this book, you've been on quite a journey. However, just because you've finished this book doesn't mean that you're finished with your work of creating patient, open, and compassionate mindful responses toward yourself and all of your experiences. Take a moment now to pause and reflect on how you'll take the work you've done here into your life:

- How will it create depth and meaning in the way you allow yourself to experience the life you've been given?

- How will it affect the way you are in the presence of others?

- How will it affect the way you look at the suffering in the world and your responses to help alleviate this suffering?

- How will it affect the way you see yourself in relation to the rest of the life process, such as the environment, the earth's resources, the things you purchase, and the foods you eat?

- What role will the practices in this book play in your spiritual journey?

Mindfulness is a way of *being* in the world. Being mindful reflects the way you respond to the ever-present flow of events and experiences in your life from a place of patience, openness, and compassion. Mindful living is how you stay present and hold yourself and your experiences with great tenderness and care, embracing your life as it is without illusion, delusion, attachment, or aggression. Regardless of your situation in life and your current circumstances, embrace the opportunity to bring the kindness and beauty within you and around you into all aspects of your life. Remember, the qualities of mindful living are ever-present; you don't have to do anything to create them in your life. They will naturally manifest as you clear away the distractions, noise, and clutter in your mind and in your life. It's similar to clearing a garden in spring to make room for the new growth to emerge.

In the practices in this book, I've endeavored to help you bring clear seeing to the influence of fear in your life. Each practice was designed to help reduce these influences, loosen the grip of big deal mind, and help you with the lifelong task of lifting the veils of illusion, delusion, attachment, and aggression. Remain alert to all of the strategies and ways of being you've developed that serve to disconnect you from your life. When you notice the urge to resort to these strategies, don't judge yourself. Simply notice what has happened, name it, and let it go. This creates the space for you to respond to the unfolding events of your life with patience, openness, and compassion. Doing so will strengthen your feelings of deep and genuine connection with everyone in your life, and ultimately with all of life. As you sense your integral place within creation, you'll understand at a deep level that mindfulness isn't just about making your life better, it also extends to making the world a place where all living beings can be happy, safe, and healthy.

Throughout your life, remember to reconnect with your pause: the pause at the end of each breath, between each word, and between each activity or step in a process. This pause is the gift that connects you to something larger. It can remind you that you aren't alone, that there isn't as much to fear as you may have come to believe, that the love and compassion that reside in your heart are to be shared with the world, and that you are deeply connected to all of creation in the most remarkable way.

Thank you for this opportunity to be part of your journey of discovery and mindful living. Take the peace in your heart into the world.

May you be happy.
May you be healthy.
May you live with ease.

Resources

HELPFUL BOOKS

Bayda, E. 2003. *At Home in the Muddy Water: A Guide to Finding Peace Within Everyday Chaos.* Boston: Shambhala.

Bein, T., and B. Bein. 2002. *Mindful Recovery: A Spiritual Path to Healing from Addiction.* Hoboken, NJ: John Wiley and Sons.

Bein, T., and B. Bein. 2003. *Find the Center Within: The Healing Way of Mindfulness Meditation.* Hoboken, NJ: John Wiley and Sons.

Bhikkhu, A. B. 1996. *Mindfulness with Breathing: A Manual for Serious Beginners.* Boston: Wisdom Publications.

Boorstein, S. 1996. *Don't Just Do Something, Sit There: A Mindfulness Retreat with Sylvia Boorstein.* San Francisco: Harper.

Boorstein, S. 2006. *Road Sage: Mindfulness Techniques for Drivers.* Louisville: Sounds True.

Brach, T. 2003. *Radical Acceptance: Embracing Your Life with the Heart of a Buddha.* New York: Bantam.

Brach, T. 2005. *Radical Self-Acceptance: A Buddhist Guide to Freeing Yourself from Shame.* Audio CD. Louisville, CO: Sounds True.

Braza, J. 1997. *Moment by Moment: The Art and Practice of Mindfulness.* Boston: Tuttle Publishing.

Chödrön, P. 2001. *The Places That Scare You: A Guide to Fearlessness in Difficult Times.* Boston: Shambhala Publications.

Chödrön, P. 2002. *Comfortable with Uncertainty: 108 teachings.* Boston: Shambhala Publications.

Cooper, D. A. 1982. *Silence, Simplicity, and Solitude.* New York: Harper and Row.

Dreher, D. 1990. *The Tao of Inner Peace.* New York. Harper Perennial.

DuPont, L. H. 2001. *Footprints in the Snow.* Boston: Journey Editions.

Finley, J. 1985. *Merton's Palace of Nowhere: A Search for God Through Awareness of the True Self.* Notre Dame, IN: Ave Maria Press.

Fromm, E. 1976. *To Have or to Be?* New York: Harper Collins.

Goldsmith, J. 1958. *Practicing the Presence: The Inspirational Guide to Regaining Meaning and a Sense of Purpose in Your Life.* San Francisco: Harper San Francisco.

Goldstein, J. 1993. *Insight Meditation: The Practice of Freedom.* Boston: Shambhala.

Goldstein, J., and J. Kornfield. 1988. *Seeking the Heart of Wisdom: The Path of Insight Meditation.* Boston: Shambhala.

Hamhill, S. (trans.). 1995. *The Little Book of Haiku.* New York: Barnes and Noble Books.

Hardy, J. 2002. *Haiku Poetry: Ancient and Modern.* Boston: Turtle Publishing.

Kabat-Zinn, J. 1995. *Wherever You Go, There You Are: Mindfulness Meditation in Everyday Life.* New York: Little, Brown.

Keating, T. 1994. *Open Mind, Open Heart.* New York: Continuum Publishing.

Kornfield, J. 1993. *A Path with Heart: A Guide Through the Perils and Promises of Spiritual Life.* New York: Bantam.

Merton, T. 1955. *No Man Is an Island.* New York: Harcourt.

Merzel, D. G. 1991. *The Eye Never Sleeps: Striking to the Heart of Zen*. Boston: Shambhala.

Merzel, D. G. 2003. *The Path of the Human Being: Zen Teachings on the Bodhisattva Way*. Boston: Shambhala.

Mitchell, S. 1988. *Tao Te Ching*. New York: Harper Row.

Nhat Hanh, T. 1987. *Being Peace*. Berkeley, CA: Parallax Press.

Nhat Hanh, T. 1988. *Breathe! You Are Alive*. Berkeley, CA: Parallax Press.

Nhat Hanh, T. 1991. *Peace Is Every Step: The Path of Mindfulness in Everyday Life*. New York: Bantam Books.

Nhat Hanh, T. 1992. *The Miracle of Mindfulness: A Manual on Meditation*. Boston: Beacon Press.

Nhat Hanh, T. 1997. *Touching Peace: Practicing the Art of Mindful Living*. Berkeley, CA: Parallax Press.

Salzberg, S. 1995. *Loving-Kindness: The Revolutionary Art of Happiness*. Boston: Shambhala.

Salzberg, S. 1999. *A Heart as Wide as the World: Stories on the Path to Loving Kindness*. Boston: Shambhala.

Strand, C. 1997. *Seeds from a Birch Tree: Writing Haiku and the Spiritual Journey*. New York: Hyperion.

Tolle, E. 1999. *The Power of Now*. Novato, CA: New World Publishing.

Tolle, E. 2001. *Practicing the Power of Now*. Novato, CA: New World Publishing.

Tomm, W. 1995. *Bodied Mindfulness: Women's Spirits, Bodies, and Places*. Waterloo, Ontario: Wilfred Laurier University Press.

Watts, A. 1951. *The Wisdom of Insecurity: A Message for an Age of Anxiety*. New York: Vintage Books.

AUDIO RECORDINGS

Sounds True (www.soundstrue.com). This multimedia publishing company offers more than six hundred titles, with many by the leading teachers and visionaries of our time. Its website is www.soundstrue.com.

Audio Dharma (www.audiodharma.org). This website offers an archive of dharma talks given by Gil Fronsdal, a Zen priest with a Ph.D. in Buddhist studies, and various guest speakers at the Insight Meditation Center in Redwood City, California. The talks illuminate the teachings of the Buddha, including discussion of mindfulness, insight meditation (sometimes called *vipassana meditation*), and loving-kindness.

MEDITATION CENTERS

The mindfulness-based stress reduction program founded by Jon Kabat-Zinn is internationally acclaimed for the teaching of mindfulness. To find a trained instructor in your area, call the Center for Mindfulness at 508-856-2656, or visit the program's website at www.umassmed.edu /cfm/mbsr.

You can also search the Web using keywords such as mindfulness, vipassana, and meditation to find centers and groups in your area with a focus on mindfulness.

References

Armour, J. A., and J. Ardell, eds. 1994. *Neurocardiology*. New York: Oxford University Press.

Astin, J. A. 1997. Stress reduction through mindfulness meditation: Effects on psychological symptomatology, sense of control, and spiritual experiences. *Psychotherapy and Psychosomatics* 66(2):97-106.

Boorstein, S. 2006. *Road Sage: Mindfulness Techniques for Drivers*. Audio CD. Louisville, CO: Sounds True.

Brown, K. W., and R. M. Ryan. 2003. The benefits of being present: Mindfulness and its role in psychological well-being. *Psychological Science* 84(4):822-848.

Cannon, W. A. 1915. *Bodily Changes in Pain, Hunger, Fear, and Rage: An Account of Recent Researches into the Function of Emotional Excitement*. New York: Appleton.

de Mello, A. 1990. *Awareness*. New York: Doubleday.

DuPont, L. H. 2001. *Footprints in the Snow*. Boston: Journey Editions.

Kabat-Zinn, J., A. O. Massion, J. Kristeller, L. G. Peterson, K. E. Fletcher, L. Pbert, W. R. Lenderking, and S. F. Santorelli. 1992. Effectiveness of a meditation-based stress reduction program in the treatment of anxiety disorders. *American Journal of Psychiatry* 149(7):936-943.

Kabat-Zinn, J., E. Wheeler, T. Light, Z. Skillings, M. J. Scharf, T. G. Cropley, D. Hosmer, and J. D. Bernhard. 1998. Influence of a mindfulness meditation-based stress reduction intervention on rates of skin clearing in patients with moderate to severe psoriasis undergoing phototherapy (UVB) and photochemotherapy (PUVA). *Psychosomatic Medicine* 60(5):625-632.

Keating, T. 1996. *Intimacy with God: An Introduction to Centering Prayer.* New York: Crossroad Publishing.

Maslow, A. 1966. *Psychology of Science: A Reconnaissance.* New York: Harper Collins.

McCraty, R. 2003. *The Appreciative Heart: The Psychophysiology of Positive Emotions and Optimum Functioning.* Boulder Creek, CA: Institute of HeartMath.

Merton, T. 1972. *New Seeds of Contemplation.* New York: New Directions Books.

Nhat Hanh, T. 2001. *Anger: Wisdom for Cooling the Flames.* New York: Riverhead Books.

Page, C. 1992. *Frontiers of Health: From Healing to Wholeness.* Essex, UK: W. Daniel Company.

Post, R. M., S. R. Weiss, H. Li, M. A. Smith, L. X. Zhang, G. Xing, E. A. Osuch, and U. D. McCann. 1998. Neural plasticity and emotional memory. *Development and Psychopathology* 10(4):829-855.

Rein, G., M. Atkinson, and R. McCraty. 1995. The physiological and psychological effects of compassion and anger. *Journal of Advancement in Medicine* 8(2):87-105.

Ruiz, M. 1997. *The Four Agreements: A Practical Guide to Personal Freedom: A Toltec Wisdom Book.* San Rafael, CA: Amber-Allen.

Shriver, M. 2009. Interview: "Living with Alzheimer's in the family." ABC News, *Good Morning America.* http://abcnews.go.com/GMA/OnCall/story?id=7525258. Accessed May 30, 2009.

Spiess, R. 2002. In *Haiku Poetry: Ancient and Modern,* ed. J. Hardy, p. 47. Boston: Turtle Publishing.

Thomas Roberts, LCSW, LMFT, has a private practice in Onalaska, WI, where he is a psychotherapist and clinical hypnotherapist. He is also an adjunct faculty member in the department of psychology at Viterbo University in La Crosse, WI. Thomas has more than thirty years of experience in both clinical psychotherapy and personal Buddhist mindfulness practice. He is a licensed clinical social worker, marriage and family therapist, and addictions counselor. Thomas regularly presents at trainings, workshops, and retreats at the local, regional, and national levels.